HELP!
I'm Raising
My Children
ALONE

REVISED EDITION

Includes Parent/Child Discussion & Activities

T.D. Jakes

HELP!

I'm Raising My Children

ALONE

Charisma
HOUSE
A STRANG COMPANY

HELP! I'M RAISING MY CHILDREN ALONE (Revised edition)
by T. D. Jakes
Published by Charisma House
A part of Strang Communications Company
600 Rinehart Road
Lake Mary, FL 32746
www.charismahouse.com

Cover design by Pat Theriault

Library of Congress Catalog Card Number: 2001088549
International Standard Book Number: 0-88419-735-2

05 06 07 08 09   9 8 7 6 5 4
Printed in the United States of America

Dedication

I dedicate this book to all the courageous people who have chosen to raise children rather than abort them. You are already a conqueror regardless of your predicament. As you overcome new challenges you will epitomize the "more than conquerors" that Paul spoke about. You have chosen to fight the good fight. I admire you greatly, and I respect what you are doing.

I also dedicate this book to my own mother, who valiantly raised her children during many family challenges—heavy work schedules, long illnesses, divorce and finally the death of my father. For the most part my father was unavailable during my developmental years. He worked hard, he fought sickness, and finally he rested from all of his toil. To be sure, those were tough times for us all. But by God's grace we endured hardness, and these gleanings of wisdom have much to do with God's Word and His insights whispered in our ears at every junction of the journey.

You don't have to be from a single parent home to have been raised by only one parent. My parents' courage to raise their children through the tempestuous sixties has been the catalyst from which I was spawned. Heroes come in all colors, genders and circumstances.

Finally, I also dedicate this book to my wife, Serita, whose unfailing love and matchless devotion have been the burning embers that kept me warm through the cold nights of stressful conditions. It has meant more to me than my vocabulary can articulate.

This is my gift back to each of you.

Contents

Foreword

I was a young woman just out of school. Being the youngest of seven girls from a family of fifteen was within itself enough for me to learn a lot about children. We were raised in the rural areas of Marion, Alabama. The Lord had blessed me to complete my education, and I met my husband while teaching school in Hattiesburg, Mississippi. My husband, one of three children, attended college for two years and was unable to complete it because of a temporary illness.

When my husband and I started our family, he worked minor jobs with long hours for little wages. He worked for a stone setting company that traveled from place to place building large commercial buildings. I gave birth to our first child, and we began the struggle that was commonplace at that time. We moved from one city to another and finally came to reside in Charleston, West Virginia, where I reared my three children. My husband struggled to find suitable employment, and we wrestled to make ends meet. He worked so much that the children and I seldom saw him. Those were hard times. He worked several jobs trying to earn enough to support us all.

I had always wanted children, so I assumed the responsibility of raising the children alone. I truthfully had to analyze what I was working with in each child. I studied their potentials, knowing the strengths and weaknesses of each. It takes observation and prayer to be a good parent. By the help of God we made it. I want to encourage every single parent who for whatever reason finds themselves alone in the task of child rearing.

I assessed the strengths and weaknesses of my husband and myself. I knew that the children would be a composite of us both. They have a tendency to possess our negative and positive traits. Any single parent must be prepared to realize that their child is a cross between two people, not just one. The child is a cross between the man and the woman with traits of each embedded—especially when the child is raised in an atmosphere where both parents are around. I always taught that association brings about assimilation. I then had to strengthen the areas of my mate's greatest weaknesses as well as head off my own weaknesses and flaws that might be present in my children.

One parent cannot be both parents, no matter how hard he or she might try. It is impossible to be both, but you can supplement them as a vitamin does a deficient diet. The child needs to feel loved no matter what. Unconditional love strengthens your relationship with your child and helps your child to overcome defects.

The formation of my children's character began from conception. I always thought that what I did while I was carrying the children also affected them. Call it superstition or old wives' tales if you want, but I believe that a brawling mother who fights and wars through her pregnancy is more apt to have an argumentative child. While if you read and study academics, the child is more apt to be studious. For instance, I studied the Bible while carrying my youngest son. I never knew that I was carrying a preacher, but I was indeed. I think that in some ways affected Thomas's ability and interest in Scriptures. It was in him from his mother's womb.

From infancy to adulthood, children must have some consistency. I know how difficult it is to wear many hats and have many children and responsibilities. Yet you get only one chance at this. There are no rehearsals and no real encores—except with your grandchildren, whom you kiss, counsel and give back to their parents. That can be nice also.

While raising my own children there were a few rules I found helpful. I learned that listening was far better than talking. You need to be able to track and understand your children. I practiced never taking my frustrations out on them. I taught them to shoot for the top. I taught them to be all they could be. I remember telling them, "If you become a street sweeper, be the best one on the road. If you become a teacher, be the best one in the school." I guess I was a motivator to them. I tried to be one. I always taught them they could do anything if they tried hard enough. When I hear my son speak, I hear that confidence and boldness coming through him. I must admit, I am proud of my children.

It is my prayer that you find wisdom and encouragement for your child and for yourself as you read this book my son has written. Your children will ultimately imitate you. You know the dress is no better than the pattern that was used to make it. If you are a workaholic before them, they will tend to be one also. So maybe it is better for you to take just a moment to read this book and prepare yourself for the greatest adventure of your life. It is like being on a ride at the carnival: There will be peaks and valleys as you go along. But remember you only get one ride, so make it count. Tomorrow it will all be over. Take it from a woman who knows: Whatever you deposit today will be your only withdrawal tomorrow.

—ODITH P. JAKES
MOTHER OF T. D. JAKES

CHAPTER 1

Shattered
Dreams

WE MUST ALL LEARN THE ART OF TAKING RISKS. THERE ARE NO GUARANTEES. NO, DREAMS DO NOT ALWAYS COME TRUE. BUT JUST BECAUSE YOURS DID NOT COME TRUE DOESN'T MEAN THAT YOUR CHILDREN'S CAN'T. ONE OF THE GREAT THINGS I LOVE ABOUT OUR FAITH IS THE FACT THAT OUR GOD RAISES THE DEAD.

Hear, O Israel: The LORD our God, the LORD is one! You shall love the LORD your God with all your heart, with all your soul, and with all your strength. And these words which I command you today shall be in your heart. You shall teach them diligently to your children, and shall talk of them when you sit in your house, when you walk by the way, when you lie down, and when you rise up. You shall bind them as a sign on your hand, and they shall be as frontlets between your eyes. You shall write them on the doorposts of your house and on your gates.

So it shall be, when the LORD your God brings you into the land of which He swore to your fathers, to Abraham, Isaac, and Jacob, to give you large and beautiful cities which you did not build, houses full of all good things, which you did not fill, hewn-out wells which you did not dig, vineyards and olive trees which you did not plant—when you have eaten and are full—then beware, lest you forget the LORD who brought you out of the land of Egypt, from the house of bondage.

—DEUTERONOMY 6:4–12, NKJV

The parent whose
dream has been shattered by the loss
of a spouse by death or divorce can, with God, teach
his or her children to realize their dreams.

Come and step behind the curtains of a draped
life and see the inner workings that are hidden
from view in the home of a so-called American
family. This is a voyage, an expedition into the inner
annals of a relationship. I would dare not embark on
this voyage except for the fact that so much brokenness exists as a result of this subject being too often
shared and too little discussed. I am speaking of the
shattered family.

This is a difficult thing to discuss because it is a trilogy full of pain and misunderstanding. This trilogy has
different perspectives. One is the perspective of the
husband or father. The perspective of the wife or
mother must also be considered. Generally neither
one is all right nor all wrong, and there is always vari-
ance in their accounts of the same event. The last perspective is the most devastating of all: that of the
children whose young minds are often bruised by the
emotional blow of warfare in the house. No hostages,

no negotiations. The war is over, the house is in ruins and life is never quite the same again. It is a trilogy of pain.

I remember hazily through the blurred scope of a child an event that turned out to be prophetic in our family destiny. I was but four or five years old, living with two other siblings and my parents in a two-bedroom house. My parents were rather poor, but it was not the kind of poverty that required sympathy. Our poverty was veiled by the fact that we were living like most of our neighbors. We were therefore oblivious to the fact that other Americans were eating real eggs rather than powdered ones. I never noticed that I wore little homemade shirts while the other children from more affluent neighborhoods wore brand-name clothes to school. It never crossed my mind that spaghetti should have meatballs. In short, we were together, and consequently we were happy.

Beneath this canopy of pseudo normalcy, I watched the unveiling of a life that would be both rewarding and painful. I watched through the eyes of a child. I was the little end of the triangle, a toddler who toddled into shocking challenge but ultimate success.

I remember that my robust father's arms looked like hams, and his voice sounded like thunder. To me he walked like Thor, the Greek god. To me he was the Hercules who came on television after the eleven o'clock news. He worked all the time to provide the plain menu and the broken furniture, which seemed comfortable enough from my then elementary point of reference.

One night as he staggered into the our little kitchen exhausted and half asleep from long hours of work, an event happened that almost foretold what we would later face as a family. He opened the antiquated Frigidaire whose large motor buzzed all the time. It was the kind of refrigerator whose big bright chrome handle pulled down and unclasped a heavy door that came open like a bank vault.

He was in search of the big glass jug that was delivered weekly to the front porch. This flask-shaped milk jar was made of glass and was sealed with an aluminum top that brightly displayed the logo of the company that produced it. It was a heavy jar, and on this particular occasion it was covered with frost. That refrigerator, used when we bought it, forever seemed to need defrosting.

My father grasped that jar with tired, overworked hands to get a drink of milk before he was off to work again. He thought he held it tightly enough, but he was wrong. It slipped from his hands and plummeted to the floor. He screamed, and blood gushed from his lacerated foot like an artesian well. The glass shattered into a million milky pieces, leaping into the air like the burning embers of fireworks before they cascade to the ground. The milk was lost, the man was bleeding and glass fragments were everywhere.

Little did we know that later our home would slip from his grip just as that milk jar had and that we three children would watch as our family and our parents' marriage would explode in front of us, leaving scattered fragments that could never be reclaimed.

I remember how we were sweeping up glass from that milk jar for quite a while. Months later a piece of glass would turn up behind a table leg or beneath a cabinet. Likewise, we would later spend years picking up the fragments of our shattered family, and just when we thought we had it all, another piece would emerge.

Understand therefore that I speak to you from the pew of human experience as well as the pulpit of theological insight. Sit down and allow me to serve you the rich broth of multiple experiences along with the seasonings that come from more than twenty years of ministry. As an experienced counselor I have caught the many tears that flow from the broken hearts of people who need desperately to talk to someone who cares about someone who didn't.

How can we evaluate the impact of a shattered dream? Who can assess the value or appraise the damage that occurs when something we longed for explodes before us? It is like the breaking of a trust or the dissolving of a corporation. But greater still, divorce causes the very blood of our most intimate identities to spill out of our personality and lay spoiled on the floor.

THE MARRIAGE IDEAL

Romance is the twinkle in the eyes of little girls who listen to fairy tales. It is a wonderment that embeds itself in the hearts of these little princesses, an awe that fuels their thinking that a fallen handkerchief from a tower of distress will summon a prince in shining armor. Yes, he will come and swim across the moat of life and snatch her from danger.

Perhaps these wonderful yet deceiving myths help to add pressure to men who are less than princes. Perhaps they add to the disappointment of ladies who grew up not always realizing that their intended was not the prince nor was she the princess she had dreamed about as a child. Yes, unrealistic expectations lead to massive disappointment.

My generation grew up in a time in which Lucy had Ricky, Father knew best and even Samantha had Darren. We grew up when there was still morality even among the secular. I know that makes me sound old, but really I am not. It wasn't long ago that even godless people frowned upon common-law relationships and same-sex unions. Those early influences and perceptions helped to formalize our dreams. I shudder to think what dreams will be birthed from the tempestuous influences of our society today. Nevertheless, the real truth of the matter is this: Many of us thought we would get an extra large helping of the proverbial American pie and then live out the dream we thought would be ours.

I am not by any means criticizing the pattern of the perfect marriage. At that time the pattern was near-perfect. It was a flaw in the material that ruined the garment. Yes, the concept of marriage is perfect. It is when we choose damaged material that we run the risk of disappointing results.

How sad are the eyes, particularly those of women whose hearts have been crushed through the disappointment of failed relationships. I single women out because most little girls grew up playing with plastic stoves and serving imaginary food on plastic plates to invisible husbands. Most little girls grew up playing house and dressing Barbie for her two hundredth marriage ceremony to Ken.

Men usually don't grow up playing house, so remember when you marry us that we may not know how to play house very well—particularly if the wrong lines were acted out before us in our own homes by dads who disappeared or by promiscuous mothers who brought home so many men that we were respectfully taught to call them "uncles." Some little boys naively thought their families were huge!

By the time one of these young men grows into adulthood and decides he is going to be everything his father wasn't, he often finds it difficult to define in his lifestyle what was not exhibited in his childhood. Add to this montage a grown woman whose little-girl perception includes expecting Ken to ride in on a white horse and heroically snatch her from the clutches of her now villainous past. What a seething pot of trouble this becomes for two people who are ill-prepared for the reality of day-to-day relationships.

Many other assassins prey upon marriage. From pornography to the economy, the list is endless. Communication between partners becomes a boring series of trivialities as they find themselves almost strangers distancing themselves one from the other.

Some may even indulge in abusive attacks on the character, performance or even the physical qualities of the one that they once promised to love and to nurture. Then life moves hysterically as if it has been set to rapid music. It is the shocking, racing beat of a music score arranged for a thriller like *Sleeping With the Enemy*. Some of you may know the conflict that arises when you find out too late that you have been sleeping with the enemy!

NOT THE ONE

Disappointment and even rage emerge when partners come to an impasse and realize that the one they married is not the one they wanted. Sadly, despair often evolves because the irretrievable time has slipped away when the now-distanced lovers were so sure that they had found the one they would love forever. Let's face it—marriage is hard work. It is not easy to find someone who fits where you are and where you are going. The art of growing together is rarer than the flaws of growing apart.

Marriage was meant to be a covenant, an oath to God sealed with the soiled sheets of a pure commitment. It is a promise between two that is meant to be enforced until "death do us part." It is the knitting together of two agendas into one corporate destiny.

You know as well as I do, seldom can people who fail to share their deepest fears and tears come together.

Marriage is so intense that God allows us the rights of intercourse and procreation. From this sacred union children are permitted and entrusted. Holy matrimony is a clear picture for which Christ's love for the church is a gleaming reality.

> If any man take a wife, and go in unto her, and hate her, and give occasions of speech against her, and bring up an evil name upon her, and say, I took this woman, and when I came to her, I found her not a maid:
>
> Then shall the father of the damsel, and her mother, take and bring forth the tokens of the damsel's virginity unto the elders of the city in the gate: And the damsel's father shall say unto the elders, I gave my daughter unto this man to wife, and he hateth her; and, lo, he hath given occasions of speech against her, saying, I found not thy daughter a maid; and yet these are the tokens of my daughter's virginity.
>
> And they shall spread the cloth before the elders of the city. And the elders of that city shall take that man and chastise him.
>
> —DEUTERONOMY 22:13–18, KJV

The blood was a defense that attested to the fact that the marriage was legitimate. Marriage was sealed by the breaking of the hymen. That bloody sheet was proof positive that they had consummated the marriage and that the bond was predicated upon the blood itself. What a bond! Oh, that we would teach our young women not to give their blood to someone who has no covenant with them. It is a one-time opportunity.

This may sound antiquated to many people. Even

Christians often struggle with their morality and standards. It is much easier to have a strong sense of moral responsibility in areas that are constantly being inspected by other people. The challenge is to maintain character when one is all alone. That is why it is important to train up the child in the way that he should go. In the formative years when the branch is tender it is most easily guided.

Even those Christians who failed to learn these principles in their earlier years, those who suffered trauma and pain, can still benefit. If they can't get into the ring, they can stand along the sides and coach those who can. Their experiences will help the young people avoid pitfalls. They are particularly helpful when their words are seasoned with wisdom and practical applications of godly principles. Don't be afraid to admit mistakes. Young people like truth!

People need to know that marriage is not to be entered into for a tax advantage or a business venture. It is not to be entered into because of sexual need or status. It is a blood covenant between two soul mates who have made a commitment to be together. You do not have to be perfect, but it sure helps if you are committed to the cause.

In the Scriptures the young girl shed her blood on the wedding night. The young man shed his blood in circumcision. He gave his blood to the Lord. His wife gave her blood to him, and both of them were covered.

Obviously God did not design this to be a covenant that was revocable. It was not designed to be something to enter into and then leap out of at will. Anytime you go against the plan of God, there will be pain. Divorce shatters emotions and damages esteem. Divorce was never meant to be, and the Bible says initially it was not permitted.

> The Pharisees also came unto him, tempting him, and saying unto him, Is it lawful for a man to put away his wife for every cause?
>
> And he answered and said unto them, Have ye not read, that he which made them at the beginning made them male and female, and said, For this cause shall a man leave father and mother, and shall cleave to his wife: and they twain shall be one flesh? Wherefore they are no more twain, but one flesh. What therefore God hath joined together, let not man put asunder.
>
> They say unto him, Why did Moses then command to give a writing of divorcement, and to put her away?
>
> He saith unto them, Moses because of the hardness of your hearts suffered you to put away your wives: but from the beginning it was not so.
>
> —MATTHEW 19:3–8, KJV

The cleaving that occurs in marriage was meant to end in a oneness of which sexuality should only be an outward expression of an inward reality. But what an expression it is! From the warm words and tender moments of trembling hearts and the sharing of innermost needs is born a bonded oneness that is so intense that the Bible says the two have become one flesh. Not two people enjoying the pleasure of sin for a season, but one flesh.

Throughout the Old Testament the phrase the man "knew his wife" is used. This statement is a reference to marital sex. Many couples do not realize that there is a level of intimacy that should be restricted for covenant couples. It is to our covenant partners and to them alone that we trust the privilege of being "known." Why be so careful? Is it just the physical act of sex that God is guarding? That is only part of it. The whole issue is deeper than that.

Understand that when we allow ourselves to be "known" in the intimate sense of the word we can never withdraw that knowledge. We can never un-know what we know. We may not continue the relationship, but we cannot dissolve the memory. That former partner is forever walking around with privileged information about you that you cannot delete. It is indelible.

It may never be discussed, but there is a gleam in the eye. There is a glow in the smile. There is a lifelong invasion of the secrets that cuts right to the heart of who we are. What more can we give anyone than ourselves? The tragedy of divorce is that you have given your secrets away to someone who has inspected them and walked away. It is worse than death, because when a spouse dies, at least your secrets die too, and all is safe. What a violation to have been naked and unashamed with someone who is now with someone else.

Please hear me—I do not want to appear judgmental. I have expressed God's design to point out why divorce is so devastating to persons who do not easily disrobe. I am not merely speaking of the nudity of flesh but the nudity of hearts. I am not merely speaking of the biological release of energies but the tremors of inner vulnerabilities. The pain comes when someone has had all that you have, then smirked and said by virtue of actions, "You are not enough."

There is a difference between being cut by a surgeon and being stabbed by an assailant. One will give you a clean incision that is able to be sewn back and heals easily. The other just savagely rips apart what was meant to be held together.

Divorce is the ripping of a dream. It is not just an incision but a gash. It is the splintering of the present, the violation of the past and the desecration of a future. It is the shattering of a dream. Depending upon your perspective in the trilogy, your healing may take months or years. Anytime something shatters, the glass goes everywhere.

Statistics say that there are more than 3,349,000 divorced single mothers and more than 664,000 divorced single fathers in this country.* But my assignment is not merely to minister about divorce. My assignment is to catch the splintered children. Today there are more than 16,334,000 children under the age of eighteen living in a home with a mother only and more than 2,257,000 children under eighteen living with a father only.** These children's hearts often get damaged in the ripping apart of their parents who all too often get preoccupied with their own vicious war against each other.

Tragically many children have become weapons used by brokenhearted people who have nothing left that the other person wants except a visit from a child. This visit is often withheld because the companions are interested in causing as much pain to their now-estranged lovers as they have felt themselves. The wounded shoot the wounded, using the child as the weapon. What these parents do not realize is that whenever a weapon is fired, the ammunition doesn't just destroy its target. In the process the ammunition is itself destroyed. Please, please let's save the children.

While you are in the process of sweeping up all the glass that plummets to the floor, while you are in the slow but inevitable recuperation of a bleeding heart, be careful that you do not draw the children into the process and abuse them in frustration while you recover.

I must say that many times throughout my ministry to the hurting I have wept with grown men and women whose hearts are still bleeding, impacted and distrustful because they overheard too many conversations—conversations in which Mom now tells all about Dad or vice versa. These monologues of bitter substance spilling out betrayal and disloyalty about a spouse create confusion in the children and deprive them of the ability to trust. After all, if a parent cannot be trusted, who can? Do not teach them distrust. Yes, they may end up successful; they may even end up married, but they will always be lonely because they will lose their ability to confide in or to trust in anyone.

We must all learn the art of taking risks. There are no guarantees. No, dreams do not always come true. But just because yours did not come true doesn't mean that your children's can't. One of the great things I love about our faith is the fact that our God raises the dead. He is a God of second chances and new beginnings. It is His Word that gives us the grace to believe that all things are possible.

> For there is hope of a tree, if it be cut down, that it will sprout again, and that the tender branch thereof will not cease. Though the root thereof wax old in the earth, and the stock thereof die in the ground; yet through the scent of water it will bud, and bring forth boughs like a plant.
>
> —JOB 14:7–9, KJV

Job says that there is hope even for a new sprout to be born out of a dead stump. Please do not destroy the sprout because you have lost the stump.

Children should be the sprouts that we fight to protect. Perhaps the tree is lost, but we can work to save the sprouts. If the sprouts are lost with the tree, then all of those years are a waste. But if what comes from your union is a healthy, well-adjusted child, you have a lot. It is to this end that we pray and believe.

I am not writing to debate the legalities of divorce. I am not writing to argue for or against divorce. The tragedy for many of us is that it is too late. The stump is already dead. The tree has been hacked to the ground.

My purpose in writing is to save the sprout. Your destiny is in the seed. If you lose your children, you cut off your future. God has entrusted them to you. You are rich, and you are blessed because you have them. I would challenge you to strengthen the things that remain. Perhaps you cannot save the relationship. I hope and pray that you can. But if you cannot or will not save that, at least save the children. They do not deserve to become casualties of war.

No, dreams do not always come true. I wish they did, but they do not. But if the dream does not come true, please let's save the vision. For without a vision the people perish. (See Proverbs 29:18.) Children are a vision. They speak to our future.

Perhaps the dream has splattered and the love has leaked from it. Maybe all that you have shared with someone has been violated and you are wrestling with inner pain. In the midst of your pain realize that you have a child who needs you, a child who has been entrusted into your care. Providing food and shelter is good, but don't forget love and stability, peace and harmony. These are the milk of life. Your children will nurse at the breast of your kindness and survive the pain of the past.

I want to share with you some principles that will help you in your quest. It is possible to bring a good sprout out of a dead tree.

---

* Source: 1992 U.S. Census Bureau Report
** Source: 1994 unpublished U.S. Census Bureau Report

Discussion Questions

1. T. D. Jakes compares how his life was shattered when his parents divorced to the time when his father dropped and shattered a milk jar.

   Think about your family's experience with divorce or death. What memory of an event that happened in your family illustrates the negative feelings and emotions you have had to deal with since the divorce or death of your spouse? Describe the event and tell why it illustrates your loss.

   _____

   _____

   _____

   _____

2. T. D. Jakes asserts that "many . . . assassins prey upon marriage." What are the "assassins" that brought death to your marriage relationship?

   _____

   _____

   _____

3. Job 14:7–9 allegorizes the hope we have to a tree that has been cut to the ground, whose tender branches are left on the tree only to sprout again. Recognizing your children as the tender branches on your tree, describe how you want them to grow and find new life after the brokenness that has occurred in your family.

   _____

   _____

   _____

   _____

Shape Your Destiny Activity

MAKE A DESTINY TREE

Materials: Tree branch, plaster of Paris (or quick cement), green construction paper, safety scissors, glue, markers, empty coffee can (or clay pot), newspaper, cleanup supplies.

Note: Unless your children are older, you may want to prepare the plaster and anchor the branches in advance to avoid any health risks to your little ones.

Help your children to select one tree branch for each family member. Using the plaster of Paris, "plant" these branches in a coffee can. Help each of your children to cut out paper leaves to glue on the branches of their trees. Have them write the name of a characteristic or skill they want to be a part of their life as they grow. (Suggestions: play basketball, show kindness, teach school, be a good worker, write books, keep promises, etc.) For younger children, ask them and then write it out for them.

Guide their thinking, taking time to discuss each thing each child lists. Ask them why they chose those items to write on their leaves. Glue the leaves—along with extra green leaves—on the trees. Then take time to allow your children to pray for God to help them reach their dreams and become the people God wants them to become as they grow.

Finish the activity by saying something personal and affirming to each of your children.

Save the Destiny Trees for use in chapter nine's family activity.

Prayer

Father in heaven, thank You for creating each one of us and for placing us together in this family. Thank You for Your promise to "never leave us or forsake us." We really need to know that You are with us, and are helping us through each day. Help us to feel Your presence and to hear Your voice every day.

Sometimes, Father, we feel as though our dreams have been shattered into many pieces. Help us to look beyond those shattered pieces to see the wonderful destiny You have for each one of us.

We want to please us with our lives, Lord. Help us to become more like You every day. Help us to love each other more, to find ways to help each other out and to show kindness to each other. Teach us to look for the little ways You are guiding each of us into the specific destiny You have for us.

Thank You for showing us that we are tender branches that can bud, and flower, and bring forth "branches like a plant" (Job 14:9, NKJV). Thank You that You sent Jesus to "comfort all who mourn, to console those who mourn in Zion, to give them beauty for ashes, the oil of joy for mourning, the garment of praise for the spirit of heaviness," that we can be "called trees of righteousness, the planting of the LORD, that He may be glorified" (Isa. 61:2–3, NKJV).

We belong to You; we are Your family. In Jesus' name, amen.

CHAPTER 2

Use the Past
to Fertilize the
Future

THE DEVASTATING EXPERIENCES OF YOUR LIFE DIDN'T COME TO STAY—THEY CAME TO PASS. THE PAST IS JUST A BAROMETER THAT ALLOWS US TO ACCESS WHAT HAPPENED AND MAKE CHANGES FOR THE FUTURE. IT IS A COMPASS, NOT A MAGNET. DO NOT ALLOW IT TO DRAW YOU INTO A REPETITION OF EVENTS.

If you walk in My statutes and keep My commandments, and perform them, then I will give you rain in its season, the land shall yield its produce, and the trees of the field shall yield their fruit . . . you shall eat your bread to the full, and dwell in your land safely.

I will give peace in the land, and you shall lie down, and none will make you afraid; I will rid the land of evil beasts, and the sword will not go through your land . . . For I will look on you favorably and make you fruitful, multiply you and confirm My covenant with you . . .

I will walk among you and be your God, and you shall be My people. I am the LORD your God, who brought you out of the land of Egypt, that you should not be their slaves; I have broken the bands of your yoke and made you walk upright.

—LEVITICUS 26:3–6, 9, 12–13, NKJV

Four principles to teach your family to use
the events and circumstances of the past as stepping
stones into opportunities to experience the glorious
future God has for each family member

These principles I will share with you are simple but solid, and they represent the ability to bring power out of pain. It is always good to bring a sense of control back to a life that has veered off to the right and for a time seemed hopelessly out of control.

As you teach these principles to your children they will be reinforced in you. Your children are the third part of the trilogy. Help them to gather wisdom out of the tragedy. Helping them will get your mind off your own emptiness. You will find answers for yourself. You would be surprised how many teachers learn while they teach!

1. Teach them the art of accepting unexpected changes.

Most people do not accept change well. I have learned that life is a continual cycle. It is imperative that we do not spend too much time lamenting over the past. If we do, it is at the expense of our future.

21

Once life has changed unexpectedly, there is a degree of shock. After the initial shock is over and the anger and disappointment have dissipated, step over depression by making plans for the future. Planning for the future is an important announcement to your heart that you are planning to go on.

It would be unrealistic to say that disappointment is not painful. It is. But once the initial shock is over, do not allow your life to get stuck in a stage that is just part of the process. This too shall pass. Allow it to pass.

One of the opening statements in many Old Testament scriptures is "and it came to pass." That literally means "it so happened." But when I hear it, I hear something a little different. I hear it as a word of encouragement to someone who thinks that what they are going through is going to last forever. Oh, no, my friend, you are dead wrong. The devastating experiences of your life didn't come to stay—they came to pass.

2. Teach them that past failure does not prevent future success.

It's true that we are fueled by the past. But fuel only works when it is combusted into another form. Gas only fuels a car as it is burned. If the past isn't allowed to combust into something productive, it is as powerless as gas that will not ignite or wet wood in a fireplace.

People who allow their past to become a thermostat for their future will be destined to wander through the same sequence of events. The past is just a barometer that allows us to access what happened and make changes for the future. It is a compass, not a magnet. Do not allow it to draw you into a repetition of events.

Some of the most successful people in the world failed in school or lost a business. Many of the wealthy have been bankrupt or started out impoverished. This year's winner was last year's runner-up. I believe that sometimes it is the failures of the past that give us the belligerence to attack the new day with a strange tenacious spirit of relentlessness.

Do not repeat old mistakes. Do not marry the first person who seems nice to you. That would be like using the new person as a sedative to numb the pain of the past person. The new person wouldn't realize it until it was too late, but he or she would be in a relationship with someone who was still in a relationship with the past. The new person would just be an antidepressant used to numb the pain.

How wise it is to learn the appreciation of making excellent decisions. For I, like many other men before me, believe that life is the end result of a series of decisions. If we are going to change the results, we must change the decisions.

The pure fact is that we can't get on with our lives until we let go of our pasts. But once we let go, our dance cards are open and anything is possible.

Teach your children the art of capitalizing on failure rather than succumbing to it. After these experiences you may be a better parent than you were before. It is always sad to miss the influence of the other parent. The pain you have been through may make you more concentrated than you were when you had help. We are going to discuss techniques that will help you employ the assistance of others around you even if the companion you thought would be with you has abandoned you and your child.

Warning: If your ex-companion has not abandoned the child, do not allow your pain to make you use the child as a pawn. Make sure that your child knows that *you* are the one who is divorced—not the child!

P.S. Make sure that you know that also. It is possible to divorce the parent and still be in love with the child. Please do not deny your child the right to have the other parent. Even if your spouse was a lousy companion and unfaithful to you, that doesn't always mean that he or she is not a faithful parent.

3. Teach them to love imperfect people.

Yes, love is a risk, but it is still worth it. Hearing you say that will help your children not to become cynical and say, "I will never love." That bitterness has helped to produce a generation of pistol-packing, drug-dealing, hard-hearted children who have seen too many adult situations too soon. We must walk our children through the process of healing. It is not just you who was hurt.

In all of us there is a composite of good qualities and bad qualities. Take away the blame and you will remove the shame. One of the greatest things you can contribute to your children after a failed marriage is the reality that none of us is perfect. Teach them that if they are going to love, they must be prepared to love flawed people.

Teach your children that Ozzie and Harriet were actors. Teach them that Barbie and Ken are dolls. Teach them that when we love people, we must love the areas that they excel in and yet be prepared to tolerate the areas that are still under construction. It will save them so much disappointment to know that all of us will disappoint each other. The truth is, we often disappoint ourselves. Yet if we are going to love anyone, we must be prepared to have an "anyway" love—a love that says, "I love you anyway."

Teach them that if they meet someone whom they feel they have to change in order to love, then that person is not the one. For when love is right, we are prepared to live with strengths and weaknesses all in the same house. It is amazing, but love seems to cover the flaws. Covering them doesn't mean that you are not aware of them; it just means that the covenant is strong enough to cover the accident—like an insurance policy that is strong enough to cover a driver who made a mistake.

> Above all, love each other deeply, because love covers over a multitude of sins.
> —1 PETER 4:8, NIV

No wonder the virgin covered the groom with blood. Blood covering is the only way any relationship survives. If it were not for the blood, we would not be with the Lord. As your children embark upon life, equip them with the necessity of knowing the art of forgiveness. If the bond is not strong enough to shed blood over, then that person is not the one!

Why is this important? I am glad you asked. After a traumatic divorce children suddenly realize that people can give up on each other. It's frightening for them to realize that Mommy and Daddy stopped loving each other. They wonder how that is possible.

Deeper still, many feel as though they might be the next victims. They wonder, *Suppose I don't clean my room or take out the trash. Maybe I will have to leave also.* Help your children walk through these insecurities. These insecurities may show up in depression or anger. The problem is not just the absence of the other parent. It is facing the fact that people do give up.

That is frightening for us all. That is why you should be sure that you strengthen their understanding of how it is supposed to work. Ultimately they will ask, "If that is true, why did you not stay together?" Tell them the pattern is right, but there was a flaw in the material. Tell them the truth. Tell them, "We failed."

Whatever you do, don't make the pattern the failure. Teach the pattern, but warn them that the pattern is the ideal and occasionally there will be flaws in the material. If you can avoid it, do not commit to a material that is so flawed that you cannot live with the garment of marriage. Tell the children that is what you did, but you do not want that to happen to them.

4. Teach them to turn their pain into power.

Pain is not biased. It comes to us all. Indiscriminately it comes against the young as well as the old. It attacks the wealthy and the impoverished. No race escapes its clutches. Its tentacles can reach the lofty or the lowly. Yet pain is productive.

If our physical bodies knew no pain, we would have no way of knowing when we were going too far. We would injure ourselves beyond repair because nothing would warn us that we had stubbed our toe or hammered our thumb. Yes, pain hurts, but there is a purpose to it.

God doesn't allow us to feel pain because He is sadistic. Pain allows us to know when we need to make changes. Prayer allows us to determine what those changes need to be. As we pray, the Master Physician analyzes and shares options that we can ascribe to—or suffer the consequences of our rebellion.

There are two types of pain that I want to discuss briefly. One of them is a pain that must be challenged. If a runner only ran until he felt discomfort, he would never excel. If a bodybuilder never pushed himself to do another repetition even when his arms were burning, he would never advance to the next level.

Both the bodybuilder and the runner will tell you there is also a pain that must be respected. Yes, there is a pain that announces to the body, "You are going too far. It is time to stop and rest." That pain is not to be ignored.

David said, "When my heart is overwhelmed: lead me to the rock that is higher than I" (Ps. 61:2, KJV). He meant that when his heart was overwhelmed by circumstances and pain that had become too much for him, he went to God in prayer.

Pain often becomes the fuel that strengthens our prayers. Have you as a parent—right in the midst of your pain and failure—considered kneeling by the bed with your children and asking God to help you? Your children are tender branches that can spring up out of a dead marriage. It will never happen if you do not teach your children to pray.

"How do I teach them?" you may ask. You teach them by admitting that their parents are not perfect and that they can fail, but there is a stable relationship that will not break. It is a relationship with the Lord.

Please kneel with your children and let them hear you pray, not blaming the other person but asking God to forgive you for whatever part you might have played—even if it was just the part of not using enough caution in choosing a marriage partner. Lay your hands on your children. Put your arms around them and lead them to the Rock that never fails.

I am a witness that He can whisper more to them in the night than all that you have explained to them in the light. To Him you are all just little children who need a rest. Rest in Him.

The bad news is, He knows your deepest flaw. The good news is, He loves you "anyway." My counsel to His younger children and His older children is simply stated but deeply conveyed: Rest in Him.

Discussion Questions

1. The author indicates that many Old Testament scriptures begin with the words "and it came to pass." He goes on to state: "I hear it as a word of encouragement to someone who thinks that what they are going through is going to last forever. Oh, no, my friend, you are dead wrong. The devastating experiences of your life didn't come to stay—they came to pass."

   On the lines below, list the major stressful events you are presently facing. As you write each one down, whisper a prayer that says, "Thank You, Lord, that this thing has not come to stay—it came to pass out of my life."

   _____

   _____

   _____

   _____

   _____

2. T. D. Jakes says, "Teach your children the art of capitalizing on failure rather than succumbing to it." Look at each of the items you listed in question one. On the lines below, state how you can use each item listed as a stepping stone to success. (You may want to list the lesson you learned from it, the opportunity it brought to you or some other positive outcome from what appeared to be a failure.)

   _____

   _____

   _____

   _____

   _____

   _____

3. Ahh! The dilemma of imperfect people! The author says, "In all of us there is a composite of good qualities and bad qualities." He advises us to teach our children that "if they are going to love, they must be prepared to love flawed people."

   On the lines below, list three good qualities and three bad qualities for each person in your family—including your former spouse.

   _____

   _____

   _____

   _____

   _____

4. We learned in this chapter that "pain allows us to know when we need to make changes." Using the same list of major stresses that you used in questions one and two, now create a plan—and a goal date—for how you can implement the action necessary to turn a failure or stress into a stepping stone. Outline specifically the actions you will take, step by step. Give the date you decide will be an evidence of your success with each step.

   _____

   _____

   _____

   _____

   _____

Shape Your Destiny Activity

OPPORTUNITY PICTURE FRAMES

Materials: Heavy card stock, broken tile pieces, glue, 5" x 7" family picture

Find enough pieces of heavy card stock approximately 9-by 12-inches to give each member of your family two pieces. Help each child cut a 5- by 7-inch square out of the center of one card.

Get some pieces of broken tile in assorted colors from your neighborhood home store. (For younger children, you may want to substitute pieces of colored paper.) Allow each child to glue the broken pieces of tile around the edges of the paper with the hole in the center to make a colorful terrazzo picture frame.

When the tiles have dried, help each child place a 5- by 7-inch picture of your family between the two pieces of card stock. If necessary use heavier cardboard behind the picture and in front of the back piece of card stock.

As you work, talk with your children about the beauty of a terrazzo tile floor or a stained glass window. Explain that both are made from broken pieces. Tell them that God does the same thing with our broken lives—He makes them into a thing of beauty.

Prayer

(Be sure you have the list of good qualities in your family members in front of you when you pray today with your family.)

Father in heaven, thank You for loving us even though we are imperfect people. Forgive us for the things we do that prove we are not perfect. Forgive us when we hurt each other and when we fail to encourage each other.

Thank You for the good things You have put inside each one of us. I thank You for each good quality I see in... [name each child, one by one, thanking God for each of the three qualities you listed about that person. As you pray for each child, lay your hands upon that child.]

Thank You that You are a perfect Father. Thank You that You will never fail us. Thank You that You have promised, "For I know the thoughts that I think toward you . . . thoughts of peace and not of evil, to give you a future and a hope" (Jer. 29:11, NKJV).

We love You, Father. In Jesus' name, amen.

CHAPTER 3

The Mourning
After

I HAVE SURVIVED A BROKEN HOME. I HAVE BEEN A BROKEN CHILD, BUT I HAVE FOUND A WHOLE GOD WHO LOVES TO MEND BROKEN PEOPLE. WHATEVER YOUR NEED, HE IS ABLE TO MAKE UP THE DIFFERENCE BETWEEN THE LUNCH MONEY OF AN ABRAHAM AND THE WELL OF WATER THAT ONLY GOD PROVIDES. IF YOU LOOK UP, HE WILL SHOW YOU DIVINE PROVISION FOR YOUR EVERY NEED— EMOTIONAL, FINANCIAL OR SPIRITUAL. SING WITH GLADNESS FOR JACOB,

And shout among the chief of the nations;
Proclaim, give praise, and say,
"O LORD, save Your people,
The remnant of Israel!"

Behold, I will bring them from the north country,
And gather them from the ends of the earth,
Among them the blind and the lame,
The woman with child
And the one who labors with child, together;
A great throng shall return there.

They shall come with weeping,
And with supplications I will lead them.
I will cause them to walk by the rivers of water,
In a straight way in which they shall not stumble;
For I am a Father to Israel,
And Ephraim is My firstborn . . .

Then shall the virgin rejoice in the dance,
And the young men and the old, together;
For I will turn their mourning to joy,
Will comfort them,
And make them rejoice rather than sorrow . . .
And My people shall be satisfied with My good-
ness, says the LORD.

—JEREMIAH 31:7–9, 13–14, NKJV

God gives perfect provisions to the person who comes from less-than-perfect situations—such as the single mother whose child is born out of wedlock.

Not all single-parent homes are the sad remains of a broken divorce. I know that other circumstances lend themselves to the complexity of this predicament. Many children were born in delivery rooms where there were no male arms to greet them. Mothers whose hair had been tossed wildly in the throes of labor panted and pushed, shoving from behind the curtain of their bleeding flesh the offspring of a wild weekend, the offspring of a broken promise.

Her glazed eyes are filled with pain; her face, moist with sweat. Strangely, she looks and sounds much like she did when the child was conceived. But at that time her lips emitted sounds of undeniable ecstasy and pleasure. Her face was moist from the passion-laced embrace of an electrifying moment—a moment that seemed blissful and fulfilling, a moment that relieved frustration and allowed her to give way to animalistic delirium. Then the flesh writhed in seduction and giving. She gave herself to the moment.

35

The stars twinkled, the moon glowed and romance was in the air. Distant music donated atmosphere. There were the gentle caresses of expectant hands and the whispered compliments that met her needs. How similar she looked then to how she does now. She was in a bed then, and she is in a bed now.

But the moist perspiration and deep moaning emerging from her now are the bleating sounds that come in the mourning after. They are the pangs of a woman in delivery whose womb is filled with baby but her arms are empty of help. She is alone.

Without a doubt ecstasy has ended and the passion has abated. There is left only the erupting responsibility that enters the world with a shriek and a cry—the painful sounds that are emitted from the broken hearts of the forsaken mother and child who are left to contend with the sad remains of the "mourning" after—the mourning that comes in the morning. The kind of slow pain like a throbbing toothache. That dull throb of pain reminds us that where we are is not the best way for us. It is the dull throb that even those close to us cannot feel.

Oh, yes, the mother may be near friends who are down the hall. The faint smell of flowers may lace the air. Still, she is alone. Later in the evening, she creeps down the hallway to look into the crib. She notices the proud couple whispering and pecking on the window at that other baby. She can't help but wish there was someone standing beside her, helping her, teasing her hair. Yes, she is alone. Tired, she stumbles back down the hallway and lies down in the bed surrounded by the noise of family and friends who talk loudly to cover up the silence.

Still in the night as she lies in that cold, sterile hospital, the silence gives way to a whimper. A whimper so soft that only God can hear. He does hear, you know. She slides down into a needed sleep, her body still rearranging itself from its labor. Just before she is submerged into sleep, she feels the soft caress of arms around her waist. Strong, loving arms—but they're gone. It wasn't real. It was just the sad memory of a dissipating moment. Finally mercy comes with sleep in its hands and allows her to rest. In the morning she must prepare to take her baby and go home—alone.

At home she may experience joy. Her baby is so pretty and seems bright and intelligent. Yet, occasionally her joy is dampened by a wondering. There is a concern about finances and who will keep what life has brought her while she goes to work. There is the torn feeling of misplaced loyalties. She wants to be at home every moment and raise her child, yet she knows she must go out to be able to feed her child. She wonders what it would be like to be someone else. No time for that. She is who she is, and she has what she has. "God, help me to do it," she whispers. He hears but says nothing in response.

Have you ever gone through anything traumatic and God said nothing at all? Have you ever needed His assurance and He was silent? There are times He doesn't speak, but there are no times He doesn't hear. He hears the faintest cry of a broken heart hidden behind a brave stare and a defiant determination. He hears a sigh at seven o'clock in the evening as an apartment door opens with keys and groceries and the baby held in weary arms. He hears the screaming of aching feet and a tired back and a girl who hasn't had any quality time for herself. He hears, He hears, but sometimes He doesn't speak.

The challenge is worshiping God in the silence. It is not enough to have fellowship with Him when He is speaking. The challenge is to continue in confidence while He dwells in silence. What is it about silence that is so disquieting to our spirits? I have known people who talk nervously on an airplane to others who are virtually silent. It is almost as if silence would be a great insult to all of humanity, so others just need to hear them speak.

I have seen people say anything to break the silence, just to hear a grunt or a sigh. What is it about silence that makes the heart restless? Whatever it is, there are times when the single parent wonders, *God, where are You in the middle of this challenge? If You don't resolve the crisis...I just need so to hear the listening God speak.*

They wonder, *Is He punishing me for past sins?* They sigh, *Is He chastising me for a moment of passion?* These are questions lurking in the minds of those who feel as if life has been unkind or unfair. Exasperated with struggle and consumed with survival, even the best of us wish we had more help. What makes some single parents' plight more blistering is the deep regret that goes along with being in a predicament that could have been avoided. It is frustrating to think that poor judgment has been the mother of a lifelong commitment that could have been avoided.

No, most do not regret the child. They love the child. Many feel that the child is the only object of love that is left. *Regardless of how the baby was conceived, he is still mine. My mistake has become my miracle*, says the heart of a mother who has no one else to love.

No, it is not the child who is often regretted. It is the circumstances surrounding the child that are the challenge. It is the plight, the blistering plight that accompanies single parenting, that can be challenging. It is a challenge even for the financially secure. It is a challenge for the widow or the widower. It is even more of a challenge for the parent of a child born out of wedlock. Somehow people react differently to the mother and even the child if the circumstances surrounding her predicament are less tarnished. Little do they know that even tarnished silver can be rejuvenated and shine to its original luster.

We then must explore the discomfort for the parent whose child is born out of wedlock. There is the constant explaining on applications and forms about the absence of a father or mother, whichever the case may be. The parent/teachers' meetings to attend alone. There are the people who are cold and insensitive and the children who repeat what they heard their parents say. And the church, God's haven for the hurting, often sits in judgment rather than providing an atmosphere of acceptance and caring. The sanctimonious invite the parent to church, then criticize that parent with reminders of the past (even though the past is all the more reason for that parent to come to church!).

You must be strong, but you can make it. You can't change the past, but you can change your future. There is hope for you and your child.

It is generally the mother who faces this plight. Seldom do you find a man who takes his child born out of wedlock from a mother who would not stay. It happens but not often. Usually it is the mother who finds herself forsaken by a man who wanted her love and her sex and even her attention, but who has no time for her child. It is generally she who is left with the chilling frost of the mourning after.

Because she is trapped by regret and trapped by her love for a child whom she finds difficult to ignore, she cries out. Have you ever found yourself crying out?

Sometimes you can be in so much pain that you wonder if life is worth living.

There was a woman who found herself with much responsibility and no help. She was tossed out of a life that she had become dependent upon. She had been the object of Abraham's attraction. She had no doubt been a conquest of his lust for many nights. It is sad how circumstances can turn. Now she is turned out on her own like an old refrigerator that has lost its usefulness.

> Wherefore she said unto Abraham, Cast out this bondwoman and her son: for the son of this bondwoman shall not be heir with my son, even with Isaac.
>
> —GENESIS 21:10, KJV

She had been his mistress. Even that had a certain degree of honor. In some sordid way she had felt special. But now that euphoric sense of mystique and escapade had dissipated; reality was setting in. She was now just a woman with a baby. A woman whose shape had been altered and finances demolished. She was thrown away with no honor. Her shame is that society has never made much provision for a failed woman. Her name was Hagar. Her name meant "stranger."

Sadly that is what she had become—strange and estranged. She was excommunicated from the very life for which Abraham had acquired her, to serve as a handmaid to Sarah. She was a scorned woman left with her memories as trophies to a prize that she could not claim. She was the number one winner of a prize that could not be claimed. She had been his secret passion and the gleam in his eye. But now she was an embarrassment exiled from his life with no life of her own. She could hardly care for herself.

She was alone—or so she thought.

There is mercy for a single mother whose child is born out of wedlock, out of money and seemingly out of the will of God. The child may have been conceived out of God's sequence but not out of His providence. In His providence God keeps and sustains us.

The story of Hagar shows us her problem and her deliverance. I believe she stands as an encouragement to the woman who seldom gets encouraged, the woman whose relationship with a man has been dishonorable. Even this woman has a representative in the Scriptures. Hagar stands as a representative to every mother whose baby's name had a cloud over it. She represents the woman who had to take care of the child for whom the father only packed a lunch. What he gave Hagar was not enough to sustain her.

> And Abraham rose up early in the morning, and took bread, and a bottle of water, and gave it unto Hagar, putting it on her shoulder, and the child, and sent her away: and she departed, and wandered in the wilderness of Beersheba.
>
> —GENESIS 21:14, KJV

His child support was not enough. It carried her a little way, but it was a poor attempt given by a guilt-ridden man whose life had outgrown his need of her. Did he feel for her? Probably. Did he love his illegitimate son? Certainly. It was just that his wife had decided that enough was enough. He had made a hard choice. It was the right choice. But right for whom? Was it right for Hagar? No. It was right for Sarah. It was right for him. But the truth is that sometimes when something is done wrong, even right hurts.

He gave her a token offering—a lunch. There are single mothers all over this country who, like Hagar,

41

have been sent into the wilderness with a baby and a lunch. In some cases it was all the father had to give. In Abraham's case, it was a poor, meager attempt at guilt relief. He was a wealthy man. But even women who play with wealthy men who are not theirs end up with a baby and a lunch. Some of you have been trying to buy diapers, football uniforms, prom dresses and more out of lunch money.

I do not know whether Hagar was driven to a state of anxiety by Abraham's rejection of her or by his poor provisional skills. Whichever it was, she was in the wilderness of anxiety, and she was about to die.

I want to encourage the woman who feels betrayed and exiled. The one who feels angry and forsaken. She has been sent away, hidden down under. She is walking through the jungle of life—the jungle of starting over, of public shame or even of loving someone else's husband. While she wrestles to correct the wrong, she is living off lunch money, and she is in a state of anxiety.

Before you call the police and have Abraham arrested, remember that what is needed here is not just a check, though that would help. She has lost more than money; she has lost self-esteem and direction. She has lost focus and identity. All of her plans mean nothing. She is dealing with the mourning after.

She is so pained that she has distanced herself from her own child. Do you know that you can allow stress and pressure to distance you from the very child you are working to care for? She is so distraught that she has distanced herself from her own child. Have you found yourself being angry and moody, short-tempered and frustrated? Have you distanced yourself from your children because of the enormity of problems you face on a continued basis? Hagar did!

And the water was spent in the bottle, and she
cast the child under one of the shrubs.
—GENESIS 21:15, KJV

She cast her child away from her. She didn't kill the
child; she just cast him away. My God, look at what she
is doing to her child. She is doing to the child what was
done with her. Are you treating the child the way you
were treated? Have you been screaming at the child
because someone has screamed at you? Sometimes it
is so difficult to give to others what we didn't receive
ourselves. The thrown-away woman now throws away
her child. She is living a series of broken relationships.

All over this country we are seeing Hagars who have
thrown away their children, hiding them under the
shrubs of television. Hiding them under the shrubs of
neighborhood gangs. They are invisible children hidden from the view of stressed-out, overwhelmed parents who simply feel too depleted to pour into their
children. They are not always unloving or uncon-
cerned; many are just empty and spent and tired.

Yet there is a need that cannot be ignored. Hagar's
baby is screaming for attention. Sometimes the scream
is silent; sometimes the scream is thunderous. I want
you to understand that living in a state of denial will
not solve the problem. In fact, years later it will multiply the problem.

Contrary to the suggestion of the media, this is not
just a problem of the economically deprived. Even the
wealthy have hidden their children, though the bushes
are more prestigious. Some have hidden them in fancy
prep schools. They have hidden them behind nannies
and babysitters who have no water.

None of these so-called hiding places are negative
unless they become shrubs that we use to hide the
deeper issues of poor relationships. These substitutes

only cover them, but they do not minister to them. I know so well how hard it is to regulate your time between business, responsibilities and family bonding. But if we do not allow some quality time and depend exclusively on these bushes, whether they are the Ivy League schools or the corner basketball court, everyone will suffer grave consequences.

The answer can be as simple as insisting on an occasional sit-down dinner where all of us spend some quality time together. Sometimes we can do something together that we all do anyway, like exercising together, joining a health spa or attending a local YMCA. It doesn't have to be expensive to be effective. This will save time and still allow for relationship. Or it may be nothing but having breakfast together on Saturday or washing cars together in the yard. The key word is *together!*

At all costs we must avoid the shrubs that shade the needs of our children who are still without water. They allow us to cover deeper concerns with temporary solutions that do not satisfy the thirsting of the human heart. We all need love and bonding. Many people who are in single-parent families do not dine together or do other activities together because they do not see themselves as a family. It may not be a traditional family, but it is still very much a family. Make sure that you include some family traditions. The traditions are not as important as enforcing the fact that you are a unit.

I want you to make a commitment. Investigate subtle ways that you may be casting your children to the shrubs. It is important that you do not feel guilty— that just leads to depression and helps no one. You need to explore ways that you can consolidate your time by allowing the family tradition to center around some things that you need to do anyway. Allow your children to share your life with you. You could use some company. After all, there is nothing like building relationships with those to whom we are related. No longer can we hide our children beneath shrubs that fail to quench the thirst of our children.

We can't just baby-sit our children while drug dealers, cult leaders and hate groups are training them. I have noticed that even in the churches some of those who are teaching Sunday school or children's church do not have a real vision for the children. If we have children's ministries, we must be sure that we are quenching our children's thirst rather than just baby-sitting them while they are in church.

Churches that are not using children's church should consider it. Otherwise our children get parked on a bench like a pocketbook, listening to sermons about faith to pay bills that they do not have, heal marriages, face midlife crises and hear many other wonderful messages that are not applicable to their realities.

Well, I guess you say, at least they are in church. That is true. But the real question is stated, Is church getting in them? Yes, there is shade, but no water. Many of our children are shaded but not fed. If you are going to be successful at parenting, you must be prepared to confront things that your flesh would want to deny. We have often failed to water them. We must challenge every area of our lives that deals with our children. If we are just shading them, we must challenge ourselves to water our children or move on.

Many times single parents get trapped in the rut of thinking that if they have provided shade, they have done enough. But, dear friend, they need to be watered with the same things that you need. They need affection and affirmation and at the very least, quality time.

Quantities of time may not be realistic, but there must be good communication and quality time. Communication is the water of the relationship. No matter what kind of relationship it is, if there is no communication, things dry up.

In the exasperation of her circumstances Hagar had somewhat resigned from parenting and removed herself from the issue. Have you at times been so overwhelmed with the budgets and stresses of parenting that you have hidden your child in the bushes? Be careful that you do not allow frustration to cause you to give up on what God has called you to do. That's right—God has called you to raise that child. He has anointed you with parenthood. You are commissioned to care for that child. And by God's grace, you can do it.

Please do not fall into the trap of thinking that child care is simply a matter of money. I remember a day when children were raised with values and love in meager homes with leaky roofs and lumpy cots. There is much more involved in child care than money. Politicians have convinced us that the secret to child care is purely money. Indeed not. It is relationship. You need only talk to some of the elderly who were raised during the depression. They had less and turned out better. This is not a matter of the "lunch money" that someone gives you.

You are not depending on the lunch money. That is not enough. Even if it is enough, it is not enough. Your expense is more than money—your cost is energy, attention and affections that you do not have time for. No amount of money is sufficient. But God's grace is sufficient. Once you have done all that you can do, the rest is a matter of prayer. Trust God to make up the difference between what you have and what He can provide. He is the *allos parakleto,* which is a Greek term that means "the one who stands alongside to help." Do you need help? I do. My wife and I are raising five children together, and yet I find myself saying, "Lord, help us."

I have survived a broken home. I have been a broken child, but I have found a whole God who loves to mend broken people. Whatever your need, He is able to make up the difference between the lunch money of an Abraham and the well of water that only God provides. If you look up, He will show you divine provision for your every need—emotional, financial or spiritual. He knows where the well of water is, and only He can show you where to draw from when your heart is overwhelmed.

> And God opened her eyes, and she saw a well of water; and she went, and filled the bottle with water, and gave the lad drink.
> —GENESIS 21:19, KJV

As we explore these issues, look up and open your eyes to the perfect provisions that God gives those of us who do not come from perfect situations. The situation doesn't have to change for the provision to be allocated. Lift your eyes and see that God has a provision for every problem that may arise.

I want you to review a few areas in your mind— highlights of both Hagar's failures and solutions. The mistakes are correctable if we can point them out in time. Watch Hagar and see all of the injustices that create this scenario, yet see also how God ministers to this single parent who finds herself with a child she can't handle.

Hagar speaks a relevant and necessary sermon through her life's experiences. Wisdom can be gleaned from her that will help all of us become more effective in the kingdom. I want to point out a few illustrations that you can make a matter of prayer and meditation as you hold the hands of your own precious family.

Single parents must resist living in denial.

> And she went, and sat her down over against him a good way off, as it were a bowshot: for she said, Let me not see the death of the child. And she sat over against him, and lift up her voice, and wept.
> —GENESIS 21:16, KJV

Hagar reminds me of an ostrich—she has stuck her head in the sand, so to speak. She is in denial. She thinks that if she doesn't look, her crises will go away. You may be the only one there to look over your child, but you must look. If you do not look after the child, who will?

I know the pain that goes along with being overworked and underpaid. I know how hard it is to work endlessly and never have someone acknowledge your accomplishment. But I must warn you, the desert is no place to desert your mission. So take courage and open your eyes and your ears.

She had hoped that she would not have to hear that baby crying. She did not want to see him die. Those are two things that the enemy wants to use against single parents. He knows that your eyes are the only eyes in the house. He knows that you are deserted in the desert. He wants you to close your eyes and ears. Please open your eyes. Who is with your child? With whom is he spending his time while you are wrestling with bills and business? What time did your daughter come in, and who was that in the car? These are the things that the enemy doesn't want you to hear or see. Open your ears and eyes.

If you notice your child having a lot of extra money, you'd better start asking some questions. A little investigation might be in order. Mothers especially tend to be naive. Unfortunately you cannot always assume that he is telling the truth. Where did that bruise come from on your daughter's leg? Why did she look as if she had been crying when she came in last night? Who is that she is whispering with on the phone? No, I am not trying to make you paranoid—just aware. Yes, it's good to trust our children, but even adults struggle with being trustworthy.

It is so easy for busy people to forget to ask these questions. Unfortunately there exists a temptation to hide them under the bushes. Hiding a responsibility becomes an incubator from which a greater problem can spawn.

Furthermore, Hagar was preoccupied with her own pain. Do you know that it is easy to have a full-blown relationship with your pain? The relationship can become so loud that you cannot hear the cry of those around you. She wept because in her mind she thought her life was over. She thought her life was over because she was separated from her Abraham. What she didn't know was that she was not separated from God.

Yes, even in the desert God cares for single parents. He is there in the darkest battle you have ever known. He is there in the midst of the maze of parenting. He will show Himself strong when you have needs. He cares for you so that you may care for them.

The art of parenting requires that you pass on the compassion that you have received from Him. Parenting simply passes down from your heavenly Father to you and from you to yours. If He never gave up on you, then how can you give up on yours? Pass the comfort of His presence on to those who are depending on you. We comfort others with the same comfort we have received.

> Blessed be God, even the Father of our Lord Jesus Christ, the Father of mercies, and the God of all comfort; who comforteth us in all our tribulation, that we may be able to comfort them which are in any trouble, by the comfort wherewith we ourselves are comforted of God.
>
> —2 CORINTHIANS 1:3–4, KJV

Single parents must go after their children.

> Arise, lift up the lad, and hold him in thine hand; for I will make him a great nation.
>
> —GENESIS 21:18, KJV

This simply means that the responsibility of reconciliation rests upon the parent and not the children. It is you who must go after them. Many times parents who have given so much get frustrated and say, "I am through caring." That is not easily done because it is difficult to give up on yourself, and those children are you. If they are going to be healed and strengthened, it won't be by the government trying to sit perched on lofty benches of political grandeur, regulating the needs of the broken family.

It reminds me of the greatness of God, who was the greatest single parent, when His child Adam had fallen into sin. Adam didn't look for God. It was God who went on an all out search party for His child. The Bible says He walked through the cool of the garden looking for His child.

God has given you the ministry of reconciliation. Do not lose confidence in your God-given ability to reconcile with your child. You have the power within you to succeed. The Bible says that you have the ministry of reconciliation. As a Christian you have the ministry of reconciling sinners to God. Surely He will allow you to reconcile your own child. Just do not give up on what God has given you. You may have to go out of your way, but I believe God for you.

> And all things are of God, who hath reconciled us to himself by Jesus Christ, and hath given to us the ministry of reconciliation; to wit, that God was in Christ, reconciling the world unto himself, not imputing their trespasses unto them; and hath committed unto us the word of reconciliation. Now then we are ambassadors for Christ, as though God did beseech you by us: we pray you in Christ's stead, be ye reconciled to God.
> —2 CORINTHIANS 5:18–20, KJV

You have the power to reach your own seed. I agree with you that your child will be reconciled to God, and if there exists a breach in your relationship, I believe that he or she may be reconciled to you. I want to give you three steps that Hagar employed that every single parent can use.

1. "Arise"—Lift your own self-esteem.

You can never lift others while you are lowly. You must allow the Word of God to pull you out of every slump you have fallen into. You may be pressed down over finances, relationships or just stress. Remember that in order to raise someone up, you must be above them.

2. "Lift up the lad"—Give positive reinforcement.

The Potter never presses down on the clay; He

always raises it. If you want a positive effect, remember that you must "lift up the lad" or lass, whichever the case may be. Anyone will be drawn to someone who encourages him. No one will stay around negativism and criticism. It is important for every single parent to know that regardless of your personal state, God will empower you to lift up the lad. Many of us are mere fragments of what we could have been if we had someone to lift us up. Now realize that no one can come from the outside and tear down the child if you have lifted him up.

3. "Hold him in thy hand"—Initiate personal contact.

It is extremely necessary that you have personal contact with your own children. A warm hug, a hand, a touch seems simple, but it is nevertheless powerful. You would be surprised how effective it is just to give a warm, parental touch of affirmation and affection. Your hand scents them like sheep are scented to the shepherd. They know his scent. They know his voice. They respond to his touch. If the only time your child hears your voice or feels your hand is in criticism, he will shy away from you. Hold him in your hand. It is so essential that there be some time of bonding between the parent and each child.

If we do not receive that touch, we become dwarfed in our personal, spiritual or mental well-being. It is amazing what a touch will do. You may not be able to stop the heat of the desert. You may have to endure some circumstances together, but a touch from you can bring healing and restoration. Many single parents make the tragic mistake of trying to provide things. It is nice to give things, but it is far nicer to give a personal touch.

A gentle hand placed firmly on the shoulder can

ease the torment of labor for an expectant mother. A gentle hand can secure a wobbly elderly person whose knees are quivering like jelly. A single hand can support the traumatized victim who is being placed in an ambulance. Just a touch, four fingers and a thumb, can convey the deepest message.

Lovers have always used simple touch as a means of passing messages in crowded rooms. If they can use it, knowing that the nervous system is a communication system accessed by the body at awesome speed, what about you and your child? In the hurried frenzy of a demanding day, a moment, a touch, a smile caresses the soul like a blanket gently tucked in during the chilling ebb of a night.

It is essential that the single parent envelop the child with the kind of riches that cannot be tabulated. The rich dividend of a warm touch and a kind deed will cause you to reap benefits for years to come. Give the child the warmth that he or she needs. I have determined that if one of mine ends up in the street lying in the arms of a stranger, it will not be because my child could not find affection and affirmation at home. It will simply be his or her choice. Perhaps if you and I were more nurtured, we would not have crossed lines or made mistakes that led our generation into so many children who will grow up wondering, *Where is my dad?*

Yes, there are times that we enter into a circumstance through the wrong door, but we need not maintain poor posture the rest of the day. We can by God's grace correct the mistakes and effect a change in the world through a child who was born through a moment of weakness. I want to challenge you to love your children with all of your heart no matter how they were conceived.

Neither you nor I can change where we have been, but we can always alter where we will go. That child is wind in motion headed for an undetermined location, fueled by the training that you infuse. May the gust of wind be strong enough and the love within be deep enough that they themselves will never wake up with the challenges of "the mourning after."

I know you don't want that; nor does Christ. You cannot stop them by warning them or threatening them. Many parents who made mistakes in their pasts go overboard trying to keep their children from similar mistakes. They are not overboard in their desire, just their method. They become a sexual bodyguard. They rant and rage and embarrass the child.

While I know we must be watchful, we must also balance precaution with wisdom. The greatest fire alarm must be within the house. No one can watch for a fire from the outside and think that their watch is adequate. The smoke alarm is always placed within the house. So it is with morality—you cannot totally control it from the outside. It must be inbred early in the life of your children. It is within them that we want the bell to ring when a certain kind of touch is inappropriate.

As I move on from this area to another I want to prepare your mind for a powerful reality: Never think that you are not raising a mighty child just because you are raising him or her alone. Never allow these socially pious, spiritually impotent, religious mongrels to leave you in a state of hopelessness over a mistake that you cannot correct. They should know that you can't help what happened. You can only prevent it from recurring by the implementing of wisdom and greater discipline.

Life serves up its own chastisement. It is far greater than that which man would serve. It is the flogging of the heart and the spankings of responsibility that last a lifetime. Like anyone who breaks a law, we all serve our time. One way or another we all suffer the consequences of our own decisions.

Even in the chastisements that God Himself administers there are some lilies in the valley and rosebuds amongst the thorns. He has given you a wonderful life and a powerful testimony. It is a strength when you can wake up in the morning and stop mourning. What a joy to be able to say to yourself, *I am a survivor. I will reproduce after my own kind a child who will have my strength and the benefit of my counsel. This child shall be wiser because I have touched his life with the melancholy melody of my human song.*

Discussion Questions

1. Although the focus of this chapter is on the single mother whose child is born out of wedlock, many of the emotions that mother experiences are identical to those experienced by single mothers—and fathers—everywhere. Beside each of the concerns the author gave, listed below, give a short statement to indicate your situation in that area.

   Financial concerns:

   _____

   _____

   Childcare concerns:

   _____

   _____

   Torn feelings of misplaced loyalties:

   _____

   _____

   Thoughts about being someone else:

   _____

   _____

   Time concerns:

   _____

   _____

   Feelings of inadequacy:

   _____

   _____

2. The author states, "You can't change the past, but you can change the future." What changes can

you—and are you—making in your life to change
your situation into a more positive direction?

_____

_____

_____

_____

3. Read Genesis 16:1–10; 21:8–16. Like Hagar, sometimes we tend to distance ourselves from our children because of the enormity of problems we face
on a continual basis. As a self-discovery activity,
check each of the following items that describes
an action you have taken.

❑ Treated your children in the same negative way
you have been treated

❑ Withheld love or encouragement from your child
because no one gives it to you

❑ Lived in a series of broken relationships

❑ Failed to give your children adequate attention,
using the television for a babysitter

❑ Failed to adequately supervise your children's
associations

4. For each of the checkmarks you made for question
three, list a way that you can—and will—begin to
change that negative action for a positive one.

_____

_____

_____

_____

_____

Shape Your Destiny Activity

A FAMILY OUTING

Materials: Posterboard, paper, pencils.

With your children, discuss and make plans for a family outing. Work together to prepare a budget that will give you the money necessary for this outing. (Note: There are many things in every community that cost very little—or nothing at all—yet give wonderful opportunities for quality time together as a family.)

Be sure that whatever you choose to do together really involves spending time together interacting with each other. Tell your children how special they are to you, and talk with each one about the specific needs that child may have as you plan and participate in the activity.

When the activity is over, ask each child to draw a picture of that time together. Let the child explain the picture, telling what the experience meant to him or her. Prepare a family poster, using each picture and whatever words you choose to describe your outing together. Display the poster in a prominent place in your home.

Prayer

Father, thank You for the wonderful time our family had together on our family outing. Thank You for giving [name each child] to me. Thank You for the special love You have given to each one of us for each other.

Father, help me to find more ways to spend more time with my family. Help me to make my relationship with each family member the second most important relationship I have—and to make my relationship with You my most important goal.

Thank You, Father, that we are never alone, because You are always with us. Help me every day to pray for my children the words of Paul: "I thank my God upon every remembrance of you, always in every prayer of mine making request for you all with joy . . . being confident of this very thing, that He who has begun a good work in you will complete it until the day of Jesus Christ . . . For God is my witness, how greatly I long for you all with the affection of Jesus Christ. And this I pray, that your love may abound still more and more in knowledge and all discernment, that you may approve the things that are excellent, that you may be sincere and without offense till the day of Christ, being filled with the fruits of righteousness which are by Jesus Christ, to the glory and praise of God" (Phil. 1:3–11, NKJV).

Thank You for loving us, and help us to love You— and each other—more every day. In Jesus' name, amen.

CHAPTER 4

Momma's Baby, Daddy's Maybe?

WHAT GREATER TESTIMONY CAN THERE BE THAN THE TESTIMONY THAT IS DERIVED FROM THE LIPS OF PARENTS WHOSE SCARS BECAME STARS AS THEY ASPIRED TO SURVIVE TRAUMA. YOUR WISDOM WILL LAST A LIFETIME. DO NOT LOSE CONFIDENCE IN YOURSELF BECAUSE OF PAST MISTAKES. YOU HAVE A CHANCE TO BRING RIGHT OUT OF WRONG BY POURING STRENGTH INTO YOUR CHILD.

I remember you in my prayers night and day, greatly desiring to see you, being mindful of your tears, that I may be filled with joy, when I call to remembrance the genuine faith that is in you, which dwelt first in your grandmother Lois and your mother Eunice, and I am persuaded is in you also.

Therefore I remind you to stir up the gift of God which is in you through the laying on of my hands. For God has not given us a spirit of fear, but of power and of love and of a sound mind . . .

You must continue in the things which you have learned and been assured of, knowing from whom you have learned them, and that from childhood you have known the Holy Scriptures, which are able to make you wise for salvation through faith which is in Christ Jesus.

All Scripture is given by inspiration of God, and is profitable for doctrine, for reproof, for correction, for instruction in righteousness, that the man of God may be complete, thoroughly equipped for every good work.

—2 TIMOTHY 1:3–7; 3:14–17, NKJV

A look at how a single parent can
understand the unique struggles that face
children in single-parent homes

I want to focus on a few of the unique struggles that face children born out of wedlock. Many children in this nation are faced with the stigma of painful gossip and slander that cast a shadow on them for years to come. I want to share some points of interest that may assist those wonderful children whose fight begins before they arrive.

My use of Hagar as an illustration may seem extreme, but it was intended to show the manifold mercies of God and His ability to bring victory to the victim. As we explore this issue, realize that I have come neither to attack the mother nor to criticize the circumstances that surrounded the pregnancy. It is too late to build the wall in the middle of a flood. Those kinds of warnings should come before the pregnancy. Now we must share positive ways to love and nurture the child and strengthen the mother whose sin is no worse than any other and who is no more ungodly than the man who left her living with the problem.

While there may be a few special cases where the man takes the responsibility of rearing the child born out of wedlock, generally the responsibility rests on the woman. Sadly, many women today are taking the same irresponsible solution of their male counterparts and terminating the pregnancy rather than assuming the responsibility. There is more at stake here than respecting a Christian ethic. Regardless of the circumstances that surround the pregnancy, God is the giver of life. To denounce the hideous actions of the father is one thing, but to destroy the child because of the wickedness of the father is another issue. I choose to believe that God is the giver of life.

As we continue, you will see that God can make a tremendously successful and productive person out of someone whose beginnings were not ideal.

I write with the intent to give some sense of direction and hope to those whose early mistakes have left them reeling with the sad consequences and unique challenges that surround a situation they must constantly explain, whether on school forms or medical cards. As is true with all who reflect the attitude of the Lord, we love the little children, all the children of the world.

Tragically it must be confessed that children are becoming an endangered species. They are endangered because they are prematurely having to deal with problems and harsh realities without having the maturity to handle them. Therefore we have eleven-year-olds shooting and killing and standing in courtrooms like hardened criminals without shedding a tear. It is not natural, and somewhere parenting is to blame.

You must remember that the deposits you make in your child today are the sum total of all you may expect to withdraw later. If the account appears empty, many times it is because we have failed to make an adequate deposit sooner.

I know that some children go awry without excuse. This is reality, but they are exceptions to the normal rule of thumb. Today make a commitment to fill your children with strong godly deposits that will build their self-esteem above and beyond the stigma of being an illegitimate child. It is hard for me to use that term because that term is insane. How can a child be illegitimate? The circumstances may have been illegitimate, but the child is too "legit" to quit!

> By faith Rahab the harlot did not perish along with those who were disobedient, after she had welcomed the spies in peace.
> And what more shall I say? For time will fail me if I tell of Gideon, Barak, Samson, Jephthah, of David and Samuel and the prophets, who by faith conquered kingdoms, performed acts of righteousness, obtained promises, shut the mouths of lions, quenched the power of fire, escaped the edge of the sword, from weakness were made strong, became mighty in war, put foreign armies to flight.
> —HEBREWS 11:31–34, NAS

I know by now I have raised the eyebrows of the Pharisees who would find it distasteful to encourage anyone who had erred from the Master's plan. I am of the firm conviction that the best heroes are born out of the worst failures. I do not condone the sin—theirs or mine. But I have learned to love the sinner. After all, most of us love ourselves in spite of imperfections and blemishes. When will we learn to love others with the same grace that we allot for ourselves?

Many single parents who are not widows or widowers

have lived with a terrible stigma and disgrace that were placed on them chiefly by moralists whose values were more important to them than people. Yet God, who has the right to stone any of us, seems strangely silent at our lynchings. Could it be that He wants to give us time to remember a moment in which we should have been condemned? If He in His grace has given to us the benefit of a second chance, can we be less gracious considering our own wretchedness?

I love the Lord. He wasted no time being sanctimonious or religious. He sat with sinners. He allowed Mary of Bethany to anoint His feet while the disciples whispered about Him, questioning His spirituality. He took risks on people. I know that He did. He called fallen men and broken vessels. He used Rahab the harlot and then listed her in the Hall of Faith. Not only did He use what my mother would have called a tramp, but He doesn't even hide her in embarrassment. He mentions her right beside Sarah and other women whose spotless reputations left them no purer than the grace of God that purified Rahab.

Rahab was used to being used in the night but never honored in the light. She had been the madam of many young men's nights. In that moment she was their lover and their friend, but in the morning she was not even spoken to in public. She was used to being ignored and overlooked.

Look at God who loves her through the night and honors her in the light. He mentions her as if she is the Statue of Liberty. I guess she is in a way. She epitomizes the grace of God in action. The gospel is more clearly displayed on the faces of failed people than anywhere else. For had it not been for that sovereign grace, they know that they would never have been mentioned.

I thank Him for not being ashamed of a fallen

woman. If He could brag about her faith beside men like Gideon, then who are we to condemn those whom we would besmear with our standards of piety?

What a grace bestowed and lavishly displayed. He even mentions her occupation. He is not ashamed. He almost goes out of His way to acknowledge where she came from. You must understand that grace is more gracious when it is bestowed upon the unlikely or the unlovely. He keeps no secret that she is His in spite of it all.

You see, God is not ashamed of her past. He rather displays it. It is generally we who feel that our past is so negative and detrimental that we shroud it with guilt and bury it beneath images of success. God shows His success by pointing directly to His ability to recycle the human life.

Why is this significant? When a woman has made some immoral infraction that has resulted in a pregnancy out of wedlock, she can have suppressed guilt and embarrassment that is passed to the child. It is important as we discuss the art of single parenting that we do not become so preoccupied with the welfare of the child that we fail to minister to the parent.

I have read countless articles that suggest a mother who smokes passes nicotine onto her child even in her breast milk. In the process of nurturing her child and giving him what he needs, she inadvertently pollutes him with her own vices. In that same sense a parent who is embittered or guilt-ridden may pass on her fear and neuroticism to her own child. That is why I love God's Word, because He speaks healing to the root of our problems so that we may not pass them on to others nor live with them ourselves.

God's grace is a grace that is allocated over our past. It is also a grace that can handle the challenge of a future incapacitated by early struggles. Therefore He openly mentions Rahab and her occupation knowing that His grace was strong enough to deliver her from promiscuity to become a woman of faith. Who would have thought that she would be mentioned later in the ancestry of Christ Himself? In that same sense, who knows what God will do with you as you trust Him? Pass on positives to your child.

What a wonderful thing to be acknowledged by God. He gives His name to the nameless and legitimizes the illegitimate. No wonder the sinners loved Him. He who had every right to throw stones threw none at all. Isn't it strange that we who have no right are so tempted to be judgmental?

I pray that the same spirit of grace would reach the brokenhearted and encourage the fragmented hearts of single parents who for whatever reason find themselves with enough to worry about. They need not carry the guilt for a marriage that failed or a breach in a standard, but they can learn that God can forgive and the Holy Spirit can rebuild.

Yes, there they are, paraded on the stage of faith, applauded for their faith in spite of their path. One woman is a harlot. Her name, *Rahab,* means "broad." God broadened her future far beyond her ethnicity, far beyond her economy or society. Her people were pagan, and her city was destroyed. Yet this woman survived. Are you a survivor? Then say so. And pass that strength on to your children.

What a legacy it is when a man or woman who has survived challenge can speak that wisdom and positive information into the heart of the children. Remember to do it in their youth. If it is done early, it is called teaching and nurturing. If it is done late, it is called nagging, and it does not strengthen your bond with your children. They see it as criticism.

Rahab was a resourceful woman. Yet having her in Christ's royal family could have been an embarrassment. That is the kind of family secret that most would shy away from revealing—but not the Lord. He openly reveals that somewhere in His ancestry was a woman whose spotted past and stained reputation had been cleansed by the blood—the blood that is symbolized by a scarlet cord dropped from a window. The only way that we can escape our past is through the scarlet cord of His redeeming blood.

> And the men answered her, Our life for yours, if ye utter not this our business. And it shall be, when the LORD hath given us the land, that we will deal kindly and truly with thee.
>
> Then she let them down by a cord through the window: for her house was upon the town wall, and she dwelt upon the wall. And she said unto them, Get you to the mountain, lest the pursuers meet you; and hide yourselves there three days, until the pursuers be returned: and afterward may ye go your way.
>
> And the men said unto her, We will be blameless of this thine oath which thou hast made us swear. Behold, when we come into the land, thou shalt bind this line of scarlet thread in the window which thou didst let us down by: and thou shalt bring thy father, and thy mother, and thy brethren, and all thy father's household, home unto thee.
>
> And it shall be, that whosoever shall go out of the doors of thy house into the street, his blood shall be upon his head, and we will be guiltless: and whosoever shall be with thee in the house, his blood shall be on our head, if any hand be upon him. And if thou utter this our business,

then we will be quit of thine oath which thou hast made us to swear.

And she said, According unto your words, so be it. And she sent them away, and they departed: and she bound the scarlet line in the window.

—JOSHUA 2:14–21, KJV

In spite of her tainted past and open sin, her faith shone bright as the noonday sun. It consumed the stench of her past. She stands as a testimony to women everywhere that God can forgive the most hideous mistake by a simple act of faith.

It is this kind of faith—the faith that overcomes failures and mistakes—that becomes strength to you as you raise your children. This kind of faith pumps life into the heart of a broken parent who needs desperately to see the glory of God in her life. This is the unique heritage that is borne through affliction. It is powerful and life-changing.

Understand that as a Christian we can trust no one else to pass on the heritage of our faith to our children. It is crucial that religious teaching come from the parent or parents, and then is enforced by others. It is not just a matter of teaching them your doctrine. It is deeper than that. You must teach them your faith. Teach them why you have confidence in God, what He is able to do with a human life. Who can do that but you? It is a tragedy to fail to communicate your faith to your child. It is your heart cry that will anchor your children for the future.

Only take heed to thyself, and keep thy soul diligently, lest thou forget the things which thine eyes have seen, and lest they depart from thy heart all the days of thy life: but teach them thy sons, and thy sons' sons;

70

Specially the day that thou stoodest before the LORD thy God in Horeb, when the LORD said unto me, Gather me the people together, and I will make them hear my words, that they may learn to fear me all the days that they shall live upon the earth, and that they may teach their children.
—DEUTERONOMY 4:9–10, KJV

Oh, it is wonderful to have prayer in school. But it is better to have it in the home. Teach your children how God delivered you. Single parent, you especially must teach them how God helped you and partnered with you in parenting. It is your faith that will help them grow up with a heritage. The Jews have done so well in teaching their children their faith—not just the facts of their faith but in many cases the heart of their faith. Facts will be forgotten, but out of the heart flow the issues of life.

Do not be intimidated because you cannot articulate Scriptures or teach with an easel or a chalkboard. Maybe you don't have extra time, but this is informal teaching done with Dad at the car wash or while Mother is preparing dinner. It is a bonding of hearts, the stitches that sew a fragmented family into wholeness. Your faith is the glue that bridges the gap and mends the cord. No one, absolutely no one can tell your faith like you can. Your children need to hear you say who brought you through the dark places so that when they encounter them, they will have more than religious rules. They will have faith and confidence in God.

What greater testimony can there be than the testimony that is derived from the lips of parents whose scars became stars as they aspired to survive trauma. Your wisdom will last a lifetime. Do not lose confidence in yourself because of past mistakes. You have a chance to bring right out of wrong by pouring strength into your child.

This is the chance of a lifetime. Do not miss it by clinging to guilt, bitterness, pain or revenge. Let go of your past and seize your tomorrow. That child is tomorrow. He is destiny being shaped in your palm. Your fingerprint will be left on your child's soul. Mark him well!

As we go forward, we will discuss the effects of life on children. I want to impart some insights and wisdom from a godly perspective that will assist you in steering your family to the next level of life.

We will see that some of the greatest victories are birthed out of the most challenging adversities. I want you to know that there are no limits placed upon you or your child. Regardless of the beginning, the outcome can still be glorious.

Many parents who have older children not developing in the way they expected blame themselves. In some cases they are right. There are things that should have been done differently. However, all you can do is acknowledge your wrong and then move on. Not one of us can alter the past. Yet God can alter the effects of the past and circumvent the tragic outcome. He is a miracle-working God. He worked a miracle for you, and now He will do it for your child.

Discussion Questions

1. The author states: "I love the Lord . . . He took risks on people." Listed below are two women in the Bible who were "risks" because of their backgrounds or circumstances. Read the portions of Scripture given, and then list the risk and the benefit—their positive contribution to the work of God—of God's willingness to use these women.

   Rahab (Josh. 2; 6:17–25)

   The risk:

   _____

   The benefit:

   _____

   Mary Magdalene (Mark 16:9–10; John 20:11–18)

   The risk:

   _____

   The benefit:

   _____

2. This chapter teaches us that as Christians we can trust no one else to pass on the heritage of our faith to our children. It is our responsibility to teach our children our faith and to have confidence in God. In our busy lifestyles, this teaching must be planned if it is to happen consistently. Using the outline below, plan a one-week fifteen- to twenty-minute daily devotional time that you will spend with your children. Decide what topic you will discuss each day, what Scripture portion you will use and write a prayer to conclude. Then commit to follow your plan—and to find or develop one to share with your family on a regular basis.

SUNDAY

Topic (develop your thoughts):

_____

_____

_____

Scripture portion:

_____

_____

Prayer:

_____

_____

_____

MONDAY

Topic (develop your thoughts):

_____

_____

_____

Scripture portion:

_____

_____

Prayer:

_____

_____

_____

TUESDAY

Topic (develop your thoughts):

_____

_____

_____

Scripture portion:

_____

_____

Prayer:

_____

_____

_____

WEDNESDAY

Topic (develop your thoughts):

_____

_____

_____

Scripture portion:

_____

_____

Prayer:

_____

_____

_____

THURSDAY

Topic (develop your thoughts):

_____

_____

_____

Scripture portion:

_____

_____

Prayer:

_____

_____

_____

FRIDAY

Topic (develop your thoughts):

_____

_____

_____

Scripture portion:

_____

_____

Prayer:

_____

_____

_____

SATURDAY

Topic (develop your thoughts):

_____

_____

_____

Scripture portion:

_____

_____

Prayer:

_____

_____

_____

Shape Your Destiny Activity

Do You Like Yourself?

Materials: Posterboard, markers.

Provide each family member with a large sheet of poster-board.

Ask each family member to begin by drawing a self-portrait in the center of the posterboard. Encourage them to have it resemble themselves as much as they can. Then ask them to write the following words on the left side of their portrait, leaving room to list things under the words. "I like myself because . . . "

Ask them to write the following words on the right side of their pictures: "I don't like this about me . . . "

Allow time for family members to list three or four things on each side of their pictures. When everyone has finished, let family members share what they have written on both lists. Then ask each person to share what he considered the most important thing he wrote about himself on the sheet.

Conclude by praying as a group, thanking God for each person and for the unique ways each person was created. Pray about the things your family members did not like about themselves, asking God to show each person how they can change where possible and accept themselves where something cannot be changed. Be sure to finish by thanking God that He loves each one of us just the way we are!

Prayer

A Family Prayer Diary

Father, we thank You because You made each one of us just the way You wanted us to be. "You created my inmost being; you knit me together in my mother's womb. I praise you because I am fearfully and wonderfully made . . . All the days ordained for me were written in your book before one of them came to be" (Ps. 139:13–14, 16, NIV).

Father, it's so comforting to us to know that You have planned every day of our lives. You know every good thing—and every bad thing—that has happened or will ever happen to us. And the wonderful thing is that You have determined that those things—good and bad—are the things that can help us to become the persons You created us to be.

Help us to follow carefully the plan You have for our lives. Wake us up in the mornings with fresh revelation of what we are supposed to do...who we are supposed to be on that day. When we lie down to sleep at night, fill our dreams with visions and revelations of that special destiny You have for us.

Help us to remember Your words: "Fear not, for I have redeemed you; I have called you by your name; you are Mine. When you pass through the waters, I will be with you; and through the rivers, they shall not overflow you. When you walk through the fire, you shall not be burned, nor shall the flame scorch you. For I am the LORD your God" (Isa. 43:1–3, NKJV). In Jesus' name, amen.

CHAPTER 5

The Sins
of the Father

GOD HAS A HABIT OF USING SONS [AND DAUGHTERS] WHO WERE REJECTED. HE USED JOSEPH, WHO WAS THROWN INTO A PIT BY HIS BROTHERS AND ASSUMED DEAD BY HIS FATHER. HE USED DAVID, WHO WAS LEFT ALIENATED IN THE FIELD SEPARATED FROM HIS BROTHERS AND IGNORED BY HIS FATHER. HE USED CHRIST, WHO WAS DESCRIBED AS THE STONE THAT THE BUILDERS REJECTED. HE BECAME THE CHIEF CORNERSTONE. HE CAN USE YOUR CHILD. TAKE COURAGE AND BE BLESSED. GOD HAS A PLAN FOR YOUR CHILD.

Then they brought little children to Him, that He might touch them; but the disciples rebuked those who brought them. But when Jesus saw it, He was greatly displeased and said to them, "Let the little children come to Me, and do not forbid them; for of such is the kingdom of God. Assuredly, I say to you, whoever does not receive the kingdom of God as a little child will by no means enter it." And He took them up in His arms, laid His hands on them, and blessed them . . .

For you did not receive the spirit of bondage again to fear, but you received the Spirit of adoption by whom we cry out, "Abba, Father." The Spirit Himself bears witness with our spirit that we are children of God, and if children, then heirs—heirs of God and joint heirs with Christ, if indeed we suffer with Him, that we may also be glorified together.

—MARK 10:13–16; ROMANS 8:15–17, NKJV

Regardless of your—or your children's—
beginnings, God can use you, and them, and raise your
family to success and honor. Our Father is a King—
and we are the King's kids.

Many psychologists have wrestled for years between the theory that our behavior is determined by our genes and the theory that environment is the main contributing factor in behavior. If you believe in the gene theory, then you would look at the son of a harlot and shudder because his genes are filled with the rampant promiscuity of a wretched mother whose wild lifestyle had spawned a child. His father was some lonely stranger who turned in for a few hours of frivolity before going home for the night. He is a nameless, broken, fragmented child whose demented parents could only pass on what they were themselves.

If, however, you ascribe to the environmental influence theory, you would say that his parents' genes had nothing to do with his behavior—his environment did. Can you imagine being the son of a prostitute? The clamoring sounds of creaking beds became the lullaby that rocked him to sleep. The cursing, swearing, drunken stupor of customers were his alarm clock in the morning. He could hear the guttural conversations of his mother and her friends continually. His environment was a cesspool of degradation and despair. He had been nursed on the refuse of their debauchery and perversion. He would have seen more in his childhood than most would see in their adult dreams. He was doomed by his environment and cursed by his surroundings.

Simply stated, whether you are a follower of the gene theory or the environment theory, the prognosis is still rather bleak.

A young man whose name was Jephthah was both marred by his genes and bruised by his environment. We find his story in the Book of Judges in the Old Testament. Jephthah was the son of a harlot. Regardless of your perspective, he was the sad remains of broken lives. He would be a crushed, fragmented, deranged psychotic full of confusion and despair if you judged him by either theory.

Because we are neither gene-oriented nor environment-oriented psychologists but rather theologists, we believe in the power of God. It is that power that aborts the plans of the enemy and reconstructs the misaligned for His own divine purpose. What a wonderful God we have who is able to heal the scarred and the bruised! He does it without shame, and then He parades them in the face of the enemy who tried to destroy them and says, "See what My grace did with your attack."

Oh, hear me if you are reading this and have come from some circumstance far less than ideal. Maybe you are not the son of a harlot. Maybe your childhood nightmare is built with some other plight that I have not discussed. Still the answer is the same: God's grace is sufficient for you.

It is painful for children who face extreme peer pressure to go to school and be intimidated because they have less than an ideal family. When the other children bring their toys for show and tell and discuss what their fathers bought them for Christmas, these children stand sheepishly in the corner with no presentation to make and no father or mother to refer to. Many of them will lie. Yes, I know it is wrong, but necessity is the mother of invention. They will create an imaginary family and spin a yarn full of imagined characters that reflect the life they wish they lived.

Still, no amount of imagination can erase the harsh reality of an abused, neglected or forsaken child. It is traumatic for a child to walk up and hear other children discussing their lives at home. Some will bring up the fact that he is not from a two-parent home. Some may even say that he is born out of wedlock. It can be pretty brutal what children will say one to another.

I believe it is essential that you prepare your children for attacks. Do not allow them to hear cruel, insensitive things about their own backgrounds from strangers. It is so humiliating to hear from an enemy a fact that should have come from someone who cared about how it was administered. Though you can never control what people are going to say, you can prepare your children so they may be forearmed and thereby can overcome humiliation with answers that are a reflection of good breeding and teaching.

Some of you right now know what it is like to go through the shattered areas of a broken childhood—torn by the conduct of your parents whose problems ripped you into pieces and left you lying in the blood of disappointment. And now history is trying to repeat itself in your adult life as you find yourself raising your children through broken circumstances. But if God could use the son of a harlot, I know He can bless the fruit of your body. Be encouraged. You cannot change where you have been, but you can change where you are going.

This is the gospel that preaches good news and healing to the brokenhearted. It is a message that affirms the fact that neither your genes nor your environment has to prevail over your desire to arise and become who you want to be. You are in part the master of your own destiny. You pilot the flight.

Your life is the result of positive or negative decisions. It is wise to allow the Holy Spirit to influence you so you can be drawn out of your environment and cease to be imprisoned by the aftereffects of what some say are your genes. You are what the Word says you are. If God says you are healed, then you are healed.

Jephthah, a general of faith listed in Hebrews 11, just may have been included through the wisdom of the Holy Spirit to inform us that our wretched beginnings can be altered by the righteousness of a powerful, transforming God. Perhaps He knew there would be those who felt that their genesis had rendered them ineligible to follow their destiny.

Some parents have children in sin; then in the middle of their children's lives they suddenly get saved. I have ministered to countless parents who look back at some of the things that they did in front of their children and feel guilt. They wonder, *Is it possible to see my child overcome his beginnings and become productive when some of his habits are my fault?* Well, let me share this with you. Ideally I advocate rearing children in a godly atmosphere throughout their lives. However, many of us could not lead the children where we had not been ourselves.

Parents who suddenly get saved may have some

problems with their children. Why? Because many times the child is confused and irritated by their new-found salvation. The security of normalcy has been disrupted. All of a sudden what was all right has become wrong. Yesterday you were drinking and smoking and throwing parties. Today you are reading your Bible and praying and expecting them to follow suit. It is often these cases that leave the child full of resentment and criticism because you changed your course in the middle of the stream. Now you expect everything in the house to change.

Many parents realize that this is not always easily done. They are exasperated because they want godly homes. When they try to instill those principles, the enemy suggests that it is too late. The child is angry, the parent is demanding, and frustration abounds all around. Listen, do not be discouraged. This is a matter of prayer and requires some delicacy. You don't need a butcher on an operating table; you need a surgeon. They both cut, but one has a greater sensitivity. This will require the precision of a surgeon.

The first thing is to be fair. Admit that you haven't always been who you are. Allow the child a chance to become acquainted with how and why you changed. Do not force them to change suddenly. That didn't happen with you, and it may not happen immediately with them. Just last year you were heading your child in one direction, and then after a Sunday night service, you came home completely different. Your child may not change overnight, but though the vision tarry, wait for it. In the end it will speak and not lie.

We found the Lord in the middle of our lives. Certain patterns were already in effect. It is difficult to change directions midstream, particularly for children who have been molded in a way that now, because of

87

this newfound salvation, the parents are anxious to alter. It is right to want to change; just realize that change is not always easy for those who have not been convicted or convinced.

Many times we have found Christ at the end of some real crisis or trauma in the home. To the child religion looks like a way to medicate the pain. It looks like that because often they have not been groomed in spiritual things, and it is quite a shock to them. The home is wrecked, the marriage is dissolved, the child is confused—and right in the midst of that Mom or Dad has suddenly gone into this "Jesus thing."

Many children born out of wedlock have seen the parent dating. Some have been privy to intimate information or have observed you stumbling from relationship to relationship. They are learning from what they see more than what you say. Now all of a sudden the parade of different women or men has come to a screeching halt.

Yet the child knows that Sister Mommy, as everyone is calling her at church, has not always been Sister. He knows that Brother Dad used to have a cabinet full of liquor and a refrigerator full of beer. Now all has become puritanical, and the child is confused. This is a matter of prayer. Only God can help to heal the mistakes we made through sin.

For all parents who feel that they have done things so badly they will never be able to delete from the mind of their child the past and its scars, there is the example of Jephthah. He is significant because in Hebrews 11:31 the Bible mentions Rahab, the Old Testament tramp who finally got her life together. The next verse immediately mentions Jephthah.

Jephthah was the son of a harlot. In spite of his beginning, God turned him around and used him mightily. The next time the enemy uses your past to intimidate you about the deliverance of your child, remind him of Jephthah.

God is so awesome. He often raises the disadvantaged child higher than those who had every advantage. Remember that His strength is made perfect in weakness. The Bible teaches that Jephthah was a valiant warrior, but he was the son of a harlot. In other words, in spite of his disadvantaged beginnings, the Lord was with him.

Do you know that God can take what was against you and use it for His glory? This boy was an outcast, ridiculed in his community because of something that occurred between his parents. It had nothing to do with him. Yet God blessed him. If God can bless this boy whose childhood was wrecked by his parents' irresponsibility, then surely He can bless your child. There is a spiritual warrior in that child, and nothing about your past or his can stop God's Word from coming to pass.

> Now Jephthah the Gileadite was a valiant warrior, but he was the son of a harlot. And Gilead was the father of Jephthah.
>
> And Gilead's wife bore him sons; and when his wife's sons grew up, they drove Jephthah out and said to him, "You shall not have an inheritance in our father's house, for you are the son of another woman."
>
> —JUDGES 11:1–2, NAS

Understand that as we approach this issue I am not equating children born out of wedlock as being mothered by a harlot. That is not my intent. I merely use the story to illustrate the fact that grace can cover even the most disgraceful acts. I know that many good and decent girls fall prey to the wiles of the enemy and have children out of wedlock. For that matter, many good and decent girls have been spoiled in the streets by prostitution that resulted from hunger, drugs and other ills of our society. Whatever the case, His grace is sufficient.

Now as we explore these delicate issues, we do it knowing full well that the outcome of the child's life is not predicated upon the circumstances of the mother or father. Jephthah was the illegitimate, unrecognized child of a man named Gilead. He was mocked and scorned and denied by his half-brothers. He was off to a rather deplorable beginning, but God stepped in and turned Jephthah's tragedies into opportunities.

Jephthah was like many children in this country who are born out of the passionate loins of the elite, whose passion is far greater than their compassion. It is tragic anytime a mother or father seems to have no interest in caring for what they helped to create. To make the child suffer for the mistakes of the parent is a tragedy and an injustice.

Jephthah was forced out of his rightful inheritance. Many of you have been through circumstances in which you were not treated fairly financially. You have been left rearing a child without the financial aid of a father or mother. I know the laws are changing, but as the courts prosecute deadbeat dads for child support, they must realize that support means more than money. Having two parents provides a lot of things in addition to finances.

Recently our insurance agent increased the death benefit on my wife's policies. It was not because she is the primary breadwinner. It was because she contributes things to the children and myself that would be difficult if not impossible to replace. They are not just monetary; they are in other arenas. His reason for

increasing the policy was simple: If I had to hire someone to provide what she gives to the family, it would
be expensive and, to a degree, impossible.

My point is that she contributes much more than
money. So do I. We each contribute our unique perspective. Neither of us is totally right. It is through the
intermingling of our perspectives that the children
receive wholeness.

In my book *Daddy Loves His Girls,* I mentioned
that the woman tends to favor her sons and prepare
her daughters. She does that because she is enamored
by the boys. She doesn't have to prepare them for
manhood because she has no perspective of what it is
like to be a man. She almost seems to me too lenient
at times with them. Why do I feel that way? Because I
have a tendency to want to prepare them for what it is
like to be a man in the world today.

On the other hand my little girls, whom my wife has
a tendency to want to train and prepare for woman-
hood, seem to get away with murder with me. I love
them all, but I train the boys and favor the girls. She
trains the girls and favors the boys. Through having
two parents children get a balance between being
trained and being favored.

When you are but one parent raising a family, you
must balance your perspectives between training
sometimes and favoring sometimes. It is not easy. But
it is easier when you are aware of the need to do both.
I share these things with you so you can understand
some of the differences in our contribution to the children. When you understand them, you will know better how to pray and how to fill the gap.

Your child can be successful even with one parent.
None of us come from completely ideal situations
whether we have two parents or one. Life tends to

ensure that all of us gain some exposure to broken areas. Yet God is able to mend the cracks and span the breach that life has left uncovered. Let's continue to look at Jephthah and how God became the edge that he needed to achieve.

Jephthah was denied the community of his family. He was denied the sense of belonging. He was denied the camaraderie of brotherhood and the dignity of a family name. He was identified by a mistake made by his parents for which he was not even responsible.

Sadly, a degree of our struggle begins before we do—it begins in the situation and the environment into which we are born. Some problems are waiting for us when we come out of the womb—those obstacles we must hurdle if we are going to be effective.

The crying infant who squirms in the hands of the attending physician screams in shock as he is taken out of the warm place of provision in the womb and into the harsh light of a waiting world. Some things were in place before the child even had a chance to act. No wonder he cries with the first sucking in of air. It is almost as if he knows what he has to face.

Some face poverty and others discrimination. These issues are there from birth. Life doesn't wait to form an opinion about each individual; some prejudices and poverty are prenatal. Some of those precious children are born screaming for a father's arms that will never hold them. They will never see a graying man sit in the stands of a football field and smile warmly while his son stumbles down the field.

Some will never know their birth mother. Some will find their mother's warm body waxing cold as they are snatched out just in time. They can hear the sound of the cardiologist fighting to save a mother whom they will never meet. Worse still, some are born to mothers whose addiction has become so strong that she would sell the child for a another hit of a drug that only lasts a few seconds, thereby missing a lifetime of love and affection.

BUILDING STRONG
CHILDREN FROM BROKEN HOMES

I have seen men who could not afford to buy expensive lumber to remodel their home. They would buy the B grade two-by-fours. Sometimes they would purchase boards that bowed or had knots in them. These second-class materials cost substantially less because most men would not have the time or the skill to provide the special treatment that is needed to take these materials that admittedly had disadvantages and make them work. Yet we must realize that they would not sell them if there were no demand for them. The price-conscious consumer would rather work harder, saving what others would readily spend.

There has seldom been a time when a man took those boards and did the special firings and cuttings necessary to avoid having the damaged places disrupt the finish product, that he won't tell you proudly, "I took less and did more with it." It is almost as if he takes pride in taking the disadvantage and overcoming it through skill and patience. It is that same sense of pride that the single parent exhibits when he or she raises a child and says, "I raised that boy by myself."

Most single parents will beam with pride, especially if the child turns out well-adjusted. They will almost boast about the triumph that comes from overcoming adversity. Yes, you can take a broken home and still produce a straight, intelligent, progressive child. It will require special effort and extra attention to problem areas, but when it is over you will beam with pride and say, "I did it by myself." Just remember that God was helping behind the scenes. He helped others overcome disadvantages, and He will help you.

Always remember Jephthah, who probably had far less advantage than your child has, but look at what God could do with a broken home, a broken mother, a dysfunctional father. Those variables do not sound encouraging, but when God is in them, they still add up to success. In spite of all these disadvantages, we still end up with a whole son!

My friend Jephthah becomes a bright beacon of revelatory light in the darkness of all childhood disadvantages. His life is a sermon written with the ink of salty tears. It is a legacy to all who think they are so disadvantaged that they cannot succeed. He was the son of a harlot, a tramp, a slut. He was the rejected brother of a family who showed no interest in him. He was smeared from birth with the stain of his parents' mistakes. He was perceived as a joke and an embarrassment. They spoke about him in whispers. They hushed when he would walk by. Everybody knew he was the result of a hurried passionate moment. He was the aftereffect of a business transaction made between a slut and a client. Yet he was to be God's man of faith and power.

Only a protective parent who by nature wants only good for his or her children knows the pain that is incurred in the heart of a child who is not readily accepted by the community, the school or even the church. It is a deep pain and a bleeding wound that can cause immeasurable discomfort for the parent, who over and over again does not explain why to the child. Inside, the parent also wonders why.

That is why my friend Jephthah is so important to this discussion—he is an overcomer. He is a man of war. Perhaps he learned how to be strong walking the streets as a child. Maybe he learned his strength on the local school bus of his day. Wherever it was, he became an icon of strength and tenacity. He wielded his strength against life as if it were a foe. When he finished, he made it from the downtrodden to the highly esteemed. His flag is flown in his heart. He knows he is the child of a greater Father. He is the child of the King!

Realize, in spite of what could have been a breeding ground for great dysfunction, that he excelled by the power of God. He became a great warrior and a leader. Sometimes the best leaders are made from the soup stock of meager beginnings and adversity. God takes them through an unorthodox boot camp so they will have tenacity and staying power.

If you are raising children who have been rejected and alienated from the family to which they belong, take courage. Cover those children. Love them and encourage them. But please do not think that the lack of the endorsement of the family means that the children do not have the endorsement of God, even if they are born out of wedlock or out of the graces of their family. They may be denied by men only to find that they are accepted by God.

In fact, God has a habit of using sons who were rejected. He used Joseph, who was thrown into a pit by his brothers and assumed dead by his father. He used David, who was left alienated in the field separated from his brothers and ignored by his father. He used Christ, who was described as the stone that the builders rejected. He became the chief Cornerstone.

He can use your child. Take courage and be blessed. God has a plan for your child.

Avoid Bitterness

"What can I do to enhance the children's well-being?" you ask. Well, you can start by not majoring on who doesn't accept the children and surround them with those who do. You can compensate for others' neglect with your love. Avoid being negative about the attitude of others who should have helped. Do not allow bitterness to creep into your speech.

Bitterness is the language of people who have decided that they cannot overcome. There is no room in your heart for bitterness because you are raising a Jephthah. He is destined to arise. You must be strong and of good courage. If you aren't, your children will feel hopeless and bitter also. Or worse still, they will wonder if there is something wrong with them.

It is easy to be bitter. But you must safeguard your children against your bitterness. Get rid of it. Get on your knees and pray and ask the Father to help you. It must go. It is like cancer. It will eat up your future. You see people who are bitter always talking about the past. They end up talking about it as if it were more real than the present. That thief is robbing them blind. He is opening their hearts with bitterness, and he is stealing their creativity and their song.

Do not allow it to happen to you. I speak peace to you now. Peace in the name of the Lord. That bitterness must stop. That was then, but this is now. You must have a now. For you and your children, you must have a now life. What are you going to do with right now?

These are the questions that lurk in the minds of people who are tenacious enough to get up out of the ashes and move on. Bitterness is like running with weight on. You can do it, but you won't run far and certainly not fast. I want you to allow the Holy Spirit to remove the pain that would set upon you and destroy you totally.

Discussion Questions

1. Single-parent children will face rejection at times. It may come from friends, schoolmates, neighborhood acquaintances, strangers and even from family. The author states: "It is essential that you prepare your children for attacks . . . Prepare your children so they may be forearmed and thereby can overcome humiliation with answers that are a reflection of good breeding and teaching."

    What are the things you would *not* want your children to hear about themselves from someone else?

    _____

    _____

    _____

    _____

2. On the lines below, write the answer you would like your child to be prepared to give to each one of the things you listed above.

    _____

    _____

    _____

    _____

3. It may be that you became a believer after your children's birth. In this chapter we learned that parents who are suddenly born again may face difficulties with their children. What negative patterns are you dealing with in your children?

    _____

    _____

    _____

    _____

What positive patterns of behavior and attitude are you praying will replace the negative patterns you listed above?

_____

_____

_____

4. The author teaches that you can begin to enhance your children's well-being by not majoring on who doesn't accept your children and by surrounding them with those who do. On the lines below, list the names of three people who you believe would be excellent role models for your children. Beside each name, list the characteristics that you believe that person could help to develop in your children.

_____

_____

_____

_____

Shape Your Destiny Activity

My New Song

Materials: Paper, pencils, posterboard, glue.

Provide each family member with paper and a pencil or pens. Explain that each person will be writing a song to the tune of "Jesus Loves Me" that tells about them and their lives during the past few months.

Encourage your family to think about all the things they have learned as a result of the things they have experienced. Prompt them to write words that describe their feelings, not just the events they have experienced.

When each family member is finished with a song, ask family members to share their songs with each other. Take time to discuss each song. Then encourage everyone to work together to write a family song, describing the characteristics and qualities of your family unit.

Provide posterboard frames for each family member so each song can be framed and hung on the wall. Repeat this songwriting activity periodically to write about new feelings and circumstances that come to your family.

Prayer

Father, help me to help my children to realize how important they are to You and to me. Help me to lead them into the knowledge of all the special gifts with which they were born that they may use them to fulfill Your destiny for their lives.

Help us not to look at the negative circumstances and facts about our lives before today. From this day forward, help us to concentrate on the positive factors You have shown us that will enable us to be victorious.

Help us to remember that we are "accepted in the Beloved" (Eph. 1:6, NKJV). "Let the children of Zion [that means our family] be joyful in their King . . . For the LORD takes pleasure in His people; He will beautify the humble with salvation" (Ps. 149:2, 4, NKJV). May we never forget that we are "loved . . . with an everlasting love" (Jer. 31:3, NKJV).

May my children never forget that You have made them "the head and not the tail"; they "shall be above only, and not be beneath" (Deut. 28:13, NKJV).

We praise You, Lord, for all that You have already done—and will be doing—in our lives. "Thanks be to God, who gives us the victory through our Lord Jesus Christ. Amen."

CHAPTER 6

The Image in
the Mirror

YOUR CHILDREN WILL RECEIVE A HEALTHY SELF-IMAGE AND THEREBY HAVE THE COURAGE TO FACE THOSE ON THE OUTSIDE THROUGH THE MIRROR OF YOUR TEACHING. TEACH THEM A HEALTHY SELF-IMAGE THAT IS NOT BUILT ON THE OPINIONS OF OTHERS. YOUR JOB IS TO ENHANCE WHAT GOD HAS IMPLANTED IN THEM.

Therefore I also, after I heard of your faith in the Lord Jesus and your love for all the saints, do not cease to give thanks for you, making mention of you in my prayers: that the God of our Lord Jesus Christ, the Father of glory, may give to you the spirit of wisdom and revelation in the knowledge of Him, the eyes of your understanding being enlightened; that you may know what is the hope of His calling, what are the riches of the glory of His inheritance in the saints, and what is the exceeding greatness of His power toward us who believe . . .

God, who is rich in mercy, because of His great love with which He loved us, even when we were dead in trespasses, made us alive together with Christ (by grace you have been saved), and raised us up together, and made us sit together in the heavenly places in Christ Jesus, that in the ages to come He might show the exceeding riches of His grace in His kindness toward us in Christ Jesus . . . For we are His workmanship, created in Christ Jesus for good works, which God prepared beforehand that we should walk in them.

—EPHESIANS 1:15–19; 2:4–7, 10, NKJV

A healthy self-image is one of the most important tools we can give to our children to prepare them to face life. God has implanted that tool in our children—our job is to enhance that tool for our children to use.

Most of us would never leave the house without at least glancing in the mirror. We do that so we can inspect the image in the mirror and make sure we are at our best. We want to inspect and even scrutinize what others will see throughout the day. If the image is not right, we are not as confident as we would like to be.

In the same way, your children will receive a healthy self-image and thereby have the courage to face those on the outside through the mirror of your teaching. Teach them a healthy self-image that is not built on the opinions of others. When we allow others' opinions to determine our own self-image, we are giving them too much power.

If we do not instill the right image, our children will run into the streets looking for affirmation and acceptance. Some children tend to be more insecure and perhaps more vulnerable than others. You alone can't create your children's image, but you can ensure that proper

103

care has been taken to strengthen their self-image.

I can hear you saying, "Be specific." So here it goes. To me, building self-image does not mean lying to me about the truth. Tell me when I do poorly. That is important, or I will just see your words as cheap flattery. But also be sure to point out with fervor what I do well. Be careful to be positive and encouraging. What are some of my best features? Point out attributes that are a plus to my personality.

Please do not condemn the child for not being excellent in the same areas in which you excel. Allow the child to develop his own attributes. Your job is to enhance what God has implanted in them.

TEACH THEM THE
VALUE OF THEIR OWN OPINIONS

Peer pressure would not exist if children were taught to have their own opinions. It is important that you encourage them to like what they like because they like it. The ability for others to have too much influence over your children is dangerous. It is never wrong to differ in opinion.

This can be done by asking them what they prefer. Occasionally, it is good to solicit their opinions. If you don't, they may never have any opinions. "Which color would you like your room painted, John?" evokes in him a healthy, thought-provoking process. If you are afraid which color John will choose, rephrase it by giving him a choice between tan and blue—especially if you think he is going to choose psychedelic orange!

You may have to guide this opinion-making process, and you must develop it. If you decide everything, they will never learn how to think for themselves.

THE ART OF DIFFERING

Teach your children the art of disagreeing with others without being disagreeable.

Many relationships, marriages and jobs are destroyed because the adults in them have never learned how to disagree without screaming and fighting. They have temper tantrums that were not handled in childhood. They are the ones who blow up buildings and shoot up offices—grown children who didn't get their way. They never learned how to disagree agreeably. They are angry about being controlled and dominated.

Furthermore, most people who have nervous breakdowns could have avoided them by speaking up when they disagreed. The silent passive person has an opinion. It is just buried beneath mountains of politeness and manners. Like a belching volcano, the pressure continues to mount beneath the surface until it peaks and the hot lava flows down the sides, destroying everything in its path. Help your children to learn how to differ in opinion without being obnoxious.

Yes, there may be a few knots in the wood and a few damaged bricks, but with God's help, consistency and a little wisdom, you can succeed at the art of child rearing. Some disfiguring cannot be corrected, but it can be offset by a wise parent who seeks God. After all, He has the power to make you a wise master builder. He can take less and still do more. Who else but God could take a damaged man like Jephthah and set him up as mentor for all men under his leadership to follow?

> For we are God's fellow workers; you are God's field, God's building. By the grace God has given me, I laid a foundation as an expert builder, and someone else is building on it. But each one

should be careful how he builds. For no one can lay any foundation other than the one already laid, which is Jesus Christ.

—1 CORINTHIANS 3:9–11, NIV

If God blessed old Jephthah, the son of a known prostitute, He can bless your child also. The thing that caused Jephthah to be blessed is that the hand of the Lord was upon him. Ultimately, God made his enemies his footstool. He turned their hearts around, and those who denied him later sought him.

But it all began because he did not lose self-esteem as a result of his past. When they drove him off as a youth, he became a leader first of a band of misfits. But he was training to be a great leader for his nation. Who knows what good God can bring out of someone else's mistake?

Mistakes are not the end of life; they are an opportunity for victory and learning. Too many people spend their lives grieving over what happened in the past. No one can change what has been done. But everyone can alter drastically where they are going. You will never be able to alter your destiny or fix your future if your heart continues to bleed over your past. I say to you in the name of Jesus, "Rise up and build!"

Her children arise and call her blessed.

—PROVERBS 31:28, NIV

God is up to something in your life. This is a wake-up call. You will later eat the bread that you are preparing now. In your old age your children will either bless you or curse you. They can be an advantage to you for years to come or a constant embarrassment and pain.

No, none of us know that our children will always do the right thing. That is very true. But all you can do as a

106

parent is to provide the soil that is conducive for success and then leave the rest of it to God. If your children then fail, at least you can lie down at night knowing you did all you could. And that is what you must say because they are grown and capable of making their own decisions. That is all we can hope for. We cannot assume responsibility for the actions of others. We have no control over their ultimate decisions. Our control ends with good training. That is all—nothing else, just good training. But for God's sake, be sure you did that!

> So Jephthah fled from his brothers and lived in the land of Tob; and worthless fellows gathered themselves about Jephthah, and they went out with him.
>
> And it came about after a while that the sons of Ammon fought against Israel. And it happened when the sons of Ammon fought against Israel that the elders of Gilead went to get Jephthah from the land of Tob; and they said to Jephthah, "Come and be our chief that we may fight against the sons of Ammon."
>
> Then Jephthah said to the elders of Gilead, "Did you not hate me and drive me from my father's house? So why have you come to me now when you are in trouble?"
>
> —JUDGES 11:3–7, NAS

After all of his toil he is listed in the Hall of Faith in Hebrews 11. He is celebrated as an icon of faith and leadership. He was born out of wedlock and without a family name, but God made a name for him.

It is not enough for us to invite sinners to church if we will not teach them how to live with the results of their sin. The result of sin may be a child born out of wedlock, a divorce or as simple as an irresponsibility that resulted in the loss of a job. It may be as unfortunate as a "crack" baby who was born while the mother was living in sin. Now that you are a Christian, take what life has handed you and turn lemons into lemonade.

May I stop just a moment and say to you that you might not be a Christian. You are reading, looking for wise counsel. I want to give you the wisest counsel I know. It is simple and easy, and if you will do it, God will greatly assist you. Give your heart to Jesus. Allow Him to be Lord of your life. Incorporate His teachings and principles into your daily life. He has the antidote to what is eating at you. He will help you rear your children. He will even father you. He loves you no matter what you did. He can bring pleasure out of pain. Please, please try Him now.

He will sustain you and your fruit.

> Ye have not chosen me, but I have chosen you, and ordained you, that ye should go and bring forth fruit, and that your fruit should remain: that whatsoever ye shall ask of the Father in my name, he may give it you.
>
> —JOHN 15:16, KJV

Here Jesus speaks of fruit in general. But children are the fruit of relationship. If the relationship has dried like a blossom that has lost its luster, even if it has been carried away by the winds of new opportunities—that is tragic, but at all cost we must preserve the fruit. That child is fruit, and the Bible teaches that your fruit shall remain.

When God created Adam in the garden He told him to be fruitful. He was speaking of children. He admonished Adam and Eve to reproduce after their own kind. Your children are fruit. They are evidence to the next generation that you were here. They are proof positive of your contribution to a time beyond you and a day that you might not be around to see.

It is Satan's desire to destroy your fruit. He is a liar. With all we are we must maintain what God has entrusted to us. It is important that we war with the enemy. Do not allow crime or lust, teenage pregnancy or suicide to destroy your fruit. God has a plan for your child. I want to share with you the fact that God gives life. Sex doesn't give life; God does.

There are countless couples across this land who frequently have sex, wishing that they could produce a child. But you have already been blessed with a child. Sex did not give that child to you. Neither did sin. God is the giver of life. He has entrusted you with life itself. Your fruit shall remain.

Let's talk about some of the insects that would destroy the fruit of those who have been gifted with children and have no spouse. Each situation attracts unique attacks. I will mention some situations that I have witnessed down through the years. If you know what they are, you can better know how to combat them.

1. Rearing children in your weakness rather than God's strength

Many single parents continue to have traffic in the house. Their children are reared in an atmosphere that is full of different men or women coming and going all through the nights and weekends. These parents chastise their children for flirtations and warn them against immorality, then live in the filth of their own wanton lust. The children are repulsed by the double standards.

Clean up! Clean up! Clean up! Your child is looking at you. Those rodent affairs and relationships devour the time that you need with your children. They devour the respect that your children have for you. Yes, there is a way to meet positive persons who might become your companions. But to be sure, exposing your children to your compromise will never build character in them.

Satan may be using you to pollute the future of your child. You cannot help the mistakes of your past. But to continue to repeat them is a tragedy that can be avoided. If you are continuing to practice sin, stop it now!

I think that many single parents who have not accepted that they are now parents feel robbed of their opportunity to date and experience freedom. The Bible says that to him whom much is given, much is required (Luke 12:48). It is true. There is responsibility with child rearing. It is unavoidable. Whether you are single or married, it is still unavoidable. There are required lifestyle changes.

After we had children I was shocked to realize that when my wife and I were ready to go out, we could no longer move spontaneously. Every event required planning. If it wasn't preparing bottles, it was calling a babysitter. Sometimes by the time we had packed all the bottles and diapers and blankets, I lost the desire to go. I had to learn to share my space and my wife with someone else.

2. Passing cynical attitudes on to your child

It is terrible to grow up in a home with someone who indoctrinates you by saying, "Men are no good at all. You cannot trust them." Or, "Women are worthless, just to be used for sex." These warped, pained statements that erupt from the hearts of parents who themselves have been hurt can bruise and damage their own children.

These parents need friends and counselors. Do not mistake your child for either. Children are neither analysts nor friends. They are very impressionable blank sheets of paper that you must guard against being filled with warped ideas based on your unfortunate experience. You may not know it, but you could be cursing your children's futures by rehearsing in their ears the problems of your past.

3. Living in guilt, trying to overcompensate

Parents in this situation either buy too many things for their children, such as toys, in an effort to try to compensate for something else that they are not able to give the child, such as their time and attention. Or the opposite may be true and parents obsessively go to the extremes and deprive the child. Even some Christians do this, particularly those who are attracted to religious expressions that are so strict that these expressions govern apparel, head coverings, entertainment and every aspect of their lives. Many times people are attracted to this religious conformity since they have never forgiven themselves for past mistakes. They go overboard trying to clean up as a means of self-abasement.

Allow God to cleanse you of your guilt. You do not have to be a monk or live as if you are in a convent shut up from laughter, love and life. Your sins are forgiven by the blood of Jesus. This obsessive nagging, refusing to allow the child to be a child, trying to make them dress differently, avoiding childhood games and other normal events in an attempt to pay homage for something, should be dismissed from your heart.

Before you do anything else, accept the price of redemption as the blood of Christ. We do not need to justify ourselves or pay God back. Just serve Him practically and sincerely. That will be enough.

In addition to these three fruit-destroying insects, there are also other destructive insects such as drugs, alcohol, premarital sex, teenage pregnancy and AIDS of which I have said nothing. Child molestation has reached epidemic proportions in this country. Child abductors, child labor and many other things threaten our children. I only have spent time on the things that center around how you raise your children.

The best defense against these destructive forces is offensive teaching. Preventing things before they happen is far better than criticizing after they happen. Teach your children to avoid trusting strangers. It is a job. But thank God we have God, eh? If we didn't, we would be left to think of everything. Some poor parents try to do it on their own. Can you imagine that?

By the way, have you stopped today and asked God to help you be a better parent? Have you sought His counsel and His directions? Surely you are not trying to do this mammoth job on your own, are you?

These are all insects that swarm around your house looking for an opportunity to destroy your fruit. It will not happen. It cannot happen. The Lord wants your fruit to remain. Don't be afraid of them; just put the blood on them. The blood of Jesus is against every evil work. It is out to destroy all that would destroy you. Plead the blood over your children; have prayer with them. Do it! Don't be shy. The molester is not shy, nor is the drug dealer. Speak up!

It is possible to build strong children from broken homes. The child's sphere of societal bonds is generally his immediate family. If that family structure is broken, perhaps you can enlarge the circle to incorporate other family members. Uncles and aunts become a wonderful means of enlarging the stakes and strengthening the cords of the family tent.

I know that some caution must be used because everyone who may be related to you may not necessarily be a suitable choice for help. Additionally, many single parents have family members that seem insensitive to their plight.

Single parents work hard, come home tired and

sleep restlessly, wrapping their arms around the pillows as if they had a someone to hold onto. Even the softest goose down pillow does not ease the restlessness of a bruised heart and a tired body, a body that has not been touched for months or years. It is the dull ache of solitude. Neither makeup nor neckties can hide it from view. It is the predicament of the parent who has a lot to say and no one to say it to. I know your plight. I am praying for you.

It is His presence that gives relief. God can restore the damaged areas of the home with His presence. We must teach the children the value of His presence to fill the empty places in our hearts. Voids and thirst will come to all of us. How we quench that thirst will determine our ability to survive in this world.

Your void might be the lack of a support system. You might be feeling tired and alone. I am sorry you have to face these challenges without companionship. But you are not alone. The God of all comfort is with you. He knows so well what you are going through. He cares about the areas of exasperation. He cares about the feeling of guilt, as if nothing you do is enough. He knows that when you lie down at night, there is always something on your mind that needs attention. He knows that behind being a parent you are still a person.

He even knows about the lack of intimacy and the pain of loneliness. You care for the children; I respect you so much for that. But did you know that while you are sleeping, God is looking over you? Because you are His child, He cares for you. Now rest in Him. Remember, joy comes in the morning.

> His anger lasts a moment; his favor lasts for life!
> Weeping may go on all night, but in the morning
> there is joy.
>
> —PSALM 30:5, TLB

Discussion Questions

1. We can teach our children to value their own opinions—or we can teach them that their opinions are no good, which will destroy their self-esteem. On the lines below, write three pertinent questions relating to your life right now with each of your children that you can ask each child and then allow them to answer giving their opinions. (Example: What color shall we paint your room, John?)

   _____

   _____

   _____

2. The author suggests that we teach our children the art of disagreeing with others without being disagreeable. On the lines below give one example of a time when you succeeded at disagreeing without being disagreeable, and one example of a time when you were disagreeable.

   _____

   _____

   _____

   Now ask God to give you more opportunities to learn to be agreeable—and to teach your children to do the same.

3. T. D. Jakes lists three "insects" that destroy the good fruit with single-parent children. Beside each "insect" listed below, give an illustration of a time you allowed that insect to "sting" a family member.

   Insect 1: Rearing children in your weakness rather than God's strength.

   _____

   _____

Insect 2: Passing cynical attitudes on to your children.

_____

_____

Insect 3: Living in guilt, trying to overcompensate.

_____

_____

4. Now write down a way you can kill the effects of each insect should this happen again.

    Insect 1: Rearing children in your weakness rather than God's strength.

    _____

    _____

    Insect 2: Passing cynical attitudes on to your children.

    _____

    _____

    Insect 3: Living in guilt, trying to overcompensate.

    _____

    _____

Shape Your Destiny Activity

THE "WE APPRECIATE YOU" CHAIR

Gather your family together as a group. If possible, include extended family members such as grandparents, aunts, uncles and cousins. Sit in a circle and place a chair in the center of the circle.

Explain to each family member that you are going to take time as a family to express some of the positive reasons why each family member is important to every other family member.

Allow each family member to take a turn sitting in the "We appreciate YOU!" chair in the center of the circle. Ask each member in the circle to express at least one positive reason why that person is important to them. Encourage others to affirm each statement with expressions such as, "Me, too!" "Yes, I agree with that!" and "Oh, I feel the same way about you," as each family member mentions his or her comment.

When each family member has had a turn in the chair, hold hands and pray, thanking God for the special way He made each person in the circle.

Prayer

Father, it is as we recognize our worth to You that we can begin to walk in confidence and assurance regardless of what others may say or do. Help us to anchor our lives in Your love. Let us call out to You, as did David, "In you, O LORD, I have taken refuge; let me never be put to shame; deliver me in your righteousness. Turn your ear to me, come quickly to my rescue" (Ps. 31:1–2, NIV).

Father, even David, whom You loved so much, felt worthless to the people around him. He called out to You, saying, "I am the utter contempt of my neighbors; I am a dread to my friends—those who see me on the street flee from me . . . For I hear the slander of many" (vv. 11–13, NIV). *But he knew that You loved him, for he said, "But I trust in you, O LORD; I say, 'You are my God'"* (v. 14, NIV).

Help each of my children—and me—to know that You are just waiting to help us when we need You. No matter what happens to us—no matter what others may say or think about us—"Praise be to the LORD, for he showed his wonderful love to me when I was in a besieged city" (v. 21, NIV).

Thank You, Father, for making us somebodies in You! Amen.

CHAPTER 7

You Are My Child,
Not My Friend

GUARD THESE PRECIOUS MOMENTS IN THEIR DEVELOPMENT AND DO NOT TOUCH THEIR YOUNG MINDS WITH THE STRESS AND PAIN THAT COME WITH MATURITY AND ADULT THEMES. YOU WILL BE GLAD THAT YOU DID. LATER WHEN THEY ARE OLDER, YOUR RELATIONSHIP WILL NATURALLY CHANGE, AND YOU WILL FIND THEM MORE EQUIPPED TO DEAL WITH THE ISSUES. BUT PLEASE LET THEM SET THE PACE OF THEIR DEVELOPMENT. DO NOT ALLOW THE CHALLENGES OF YOUR LIFE TO RUSH THEM INTO A ROLE THAT THEY HAVE NOT BEEN PREPARED TO PLAY.

At that time the disciples came to Jesus, saying, "Who then is greatest in the kingdom of heaven?" Then Jesus called a little child to Him, set him in the midst of them, and said, "Assuredly, I say to you, unless you are converted and become as little children, you will by no means enter the kingdom of heaven.

"Therefore whoever humbles himself as this little child is the greatest in the kingdom of heaven. Whoever receives one little child like this in My name receives Me. Whoever causes one of these little ones who believe in Me to sin, it would be better for him if a millstone were hung around his neck, and he were drowned in the depth of the sea . . .

"Take heed that you do not despise one of these little ones, for I say to you that in heaven their angels always see the face of My Father who is in heaven. For the Son of Man has come to save that which was lost . . . For where two or three are gathered together in My name, I am there in the midst of them."

—MATTHEW 18:1–6, 10–11, 20, NKJV

In this chapter we will learn the importance
of guarding the parent/child relationship and resisting
the urge to use our children as sounding boards for the
stresses and frustrations we face as single parents.

E veryone needs a friend. A friend is that special
someone to whom we can vent our innermost
thoughts without fear of criticism. Friends are
rare; seldom can you find a good one in an entire
decade. If you have ever had a friend, do not allow anyone to disrupt your friendship. You may live a long time
before you find another one. Everyone needs a friend.

Many times those who have been betrayed, forsaken
or have lost a loved one to death are very thirsty for a
friend. It is so painful to lose someone who was there.
That someone touched your heart, carried away your
secrets and then disappeared. You are now open and
vulnerable. Vulnerability will cause you to find replace-
ments too quickly. I have learned that the idea of quick
friends is an oxymoron. It takes time to build a real
friendship. It is not easily done. It is a matter of trust.

If you have been bruised, it becomes increasingly
difficult to trust again. Lust comes back around much
quicker than trust. Loneliness unpacks its bags and

moves in. Distrust teases like the taunting of a tor-mentor. The worst kind of torture is being close to something that you desperately need but not having the ability to relax totally and receive it. Many just dive in the pool anyway and think they can rush heal-ing, but that may have sad consequences.

Sometimes it is not the physical need. It is just the need for someone to sit down and talk to when the day has finally dragged to a stop. It is just having someone who understands your silence or allows you to be blue. Many times you just need someone to sit silently with you while you look into the fire and think about what could have been, what should have been.

Friends are people whose smiles are louder than their words. Their presence is as warming as a wool blanket on a cold wintry night. They are all enveloping. They are the therapists of the poor man, the family of the rich and the confidantes of the hurting. Real friends cannot be bought, nor can you persuade anyone to love you. It just happens. It happens to those at every level of life, from young children on the playground to the aged. It happens in prisons and offices. It happens in churches and in clubs—people bonding together. It can-not be fully explained. It must be experienced.

Some people have lived all their lives and never had a friend. That is the deepest, most engrossing poverty that is known to man. The absence of friendship causes the wealthy man to throw his money in the air. What good is a painting if there is no one there to see it with you? Who cares about a gourmet dinner that can only be shared with a newspaper? The soft, titil-lating sound of music becomes noise if there is no one there to say, "That is wonderful music."

Sadly, many people have had lovers but not friends. They have had marriage without friendship and sex without intimacy. They have been touched but not held. They have been fondled but not patted. They are tired of groping hands and groping people who only want them for their talents, their wisdom, their bodies or some other favor. They are hurting, bleeding, motoring down the road of life, but the path behind them is marred by a slow trickle of cold blood. They are needy.

Some are in the church going through the motions of worshiping. They sing and dance and raise their hands, shouting louder and louder as if to drown the screaming pain of emptiness that exists behind the professional smile that used to be real. They have painted joy on their faces but could find no brush to reach their hearts. Their hearts are unpainted and peeling, exposed like bare wood. They are alone.

This is a dangerous state to be in. When an individual feels like this, anyone who pays that person too much attention can cause a deluge of feelings. Like a vine searching for something to cling to, this person reaches desperately to experience reassurance. At this stage relationships become difficult to keep in boundaries. Affairs are born out of moments of reflection that water a deep thirst for friendship.

Please do not think that everyone who ever had an affair did so for sex alone. Sometimes it starts with affection from someone at a vulnerable moment. The stress, the children, the finances, the empty bed and the problems without answers lead to unnatural affections. These unnatural affections are a result of allowing emotions to be carried away by someone new while the heart is still unrecovered from the pain of betrayal. Many times people find themselves carried away with someone who is not carried away with them.

Unconsciously many people, women in particular, have become involved with their children. I do not mean that in the vulgar or perverted sense of the word *involved*. I simply mean that the relationship between the parent and the child has become distorted and inappropriate. Parents allow themselves to shrink up as people and hide behind the many demanding responsibilities of child rearing. It has become a dangerous escape mode.

The tragedy is that they wrongly try to find a level of fulfillment that was not meant to be achieved through their relationships with their children. One of the most lethal side effects of this is the tendency to become too reliant on their children. Parents need desperately to get a better, all-embracing perspective.

I send this as an urgent telegram to the hearts of men and women whose desperation for secure relationships often takes them into displacement of affection. They find themselves so desperate that eventually they have distorted one relationship for another. They are trying to get water from the wrong well. Have you ever gone to the wrong person for the right thing? It was something you needed, but in your heart you knew that it really shouldn't come from that person.

I call it mental molestation when the parent is handling children inappropriately, violating their childhood by pushing them into a friendship that denies the children the parenting they really need. It is a thin line; crossing it is dangerous because it erodes the joy of living from a child and leaves that child with an undefined and empty concept of himself.

Whenever a parent does that, it places strain on the children. Why? Because whenever people love you, they try to be there for you. It is a problem when you ask children to be something they were not meant to be. Perhaps they accommodate you, but in their hearts it stretches them and strains what their relationship with you was meant to be. You are forcing water from them that should come from someone else.

In my ears I hear the cry of children who are being abused in an unusual way. They are being abused by parents who are expecting them to be what they were not meant to be. They can be your children, but alas, they were not meant to be your friends. It is so dangerous to pervert the relationship between you and your children. The word *pervert* means "to deviate from its intended use." Anytime you mistake your child as your friend, you pervert the relationship.

Some of the side effects of doing this is that they begin to take disrespectful liberties with you, just as parents would in conversations. I believe that is why some parents find it difficult to then go back and be the authoritative figure in the house because they allowed their role to be compromised by their need for companionship.

Parents also cast undue stress upon children by weighing them down with adult issues while they are still children. You must realize that children have their own stresses designed for their level of life. When they are bombarded with Daddy's interest in his secretary while they are still dealing with the trauma of not being invited to the junior high dance, it is unfair. It is beyond unfair. It is selfish.

No wise parent would throw the car keys into the hands of a child who still has training wheels on his bicycle. Would you abuse the child's tender frame by expecting him physically to handle undue weight prematurely? Eventually, a time will come when the child could handle the weight, but prematurely the weight becomes a curse. If you would safeguard your child's body from dangerous exertion, then why not safeguard his emotions? You need a sounding board, but the child is not to be it.

As children become more aware that you have your own problems, they lose a degree of respect for you. The hero image is broken. Yes, it does need to be broken, but not during the formative years. They need to see you as someone who can handle things. If not, they will have little motivation to discuss their challenges with you. They will become less confident in bringing their problems to you because they will feel as if you cannot solve your own issues. As you embark upon new levels of stress and dilemmas, it is important that you do not weigh down those whom you are training by discussing these problems with them.

It is abusive to ask someone to become the vent for your stress, especially when that person is not old enough to be equipped for that degree of stress. I strongly encourage you as a parent, whether single or married, to avoid communicating with your children as if they were your friends. Allow them the once-in-a-lifetime privilege of childhood. It will soon be gone; why rush it away? It will never come again. It will fade so quickly that they will wonder where it went.

Guard these precious moments in their development and do not touch their young minds with the stress and pain that come with maturity and adult themes. You will be glad that you did. Later when they are older, your relationship will naturally change, and you will find them more equipped to deal with the issues. But please let them set the pace of their development. Do not allow the challenges of your life to rush them into a role that they have not been prepared to play.

As we come to the end of this issue, I have one final

note. Our modern, relaxed attitudes toward authoritative figures is having some terrible side effects. In this age when children are encouraged to call their parents by their first names, we have become so equal with the children that they have to find a role model outside the home.

It is a tragedy when their role models are characters they see on television. They have more respect for these actors than for the parents who feed them every day. Yet it is not their fault. They must be taught. They do not come into the world knowing respect.

> Render to all what is due them: tax to whom tax is due; custom to whom custom; fear to whom fear; honor to whom honor.
> —ROMANS 13:7, NAS

I was amazed to find that my children were being taught not to say "yes, ma'am" and "yes, sir" in one of the schools where we had sent them. The teacher said, "That is not necessary; I am not that old. Just say yes or no." I was shocked that they would be so interested in being young that they would be willing to compromise a respect that I was taught was just good manners.

> Children, obey your parents in the Lord: for this is right.
> —EPHESIANS 6:1, KJV

This age has such emphasis on youthful image that it has robbed our children of parenthood, which consequently robs them of childhood. There should be a difference between the parent and the child. We are not meant to be equal in terms of relationship. Children are meant to respect and obey their parents. We have so confused them that now they are divorcing us.

I know that we should be kind and loving, but that

doesn't mean that we should not be parents to our children. It is hard sometimes, but if you want a pal, get a friend. If you want a child who rises up and calls you blessed, then be the parent and maintain that posture.

> Honour thy father and mother; which is the first commandment with promise; that it may be well with thee, and thou mayest live long on the earth.
> —Ephesians 6:2–3, KJV

If you do not teach your children to honor you, you will rob them of this precious promise.

It is not well today with our children. Perhaps in part it is because they have gained in us a friend but have lost a parent. They do not come home to Mother; they walk in the door and say, "Hi, Ann," as if you were one of the children on the playground. Their father is not Dad or Daddy or even Father. He is Richard. The tumbling of titles is indicative of the falling of respect and honor.

Do not compromise your respect or you will lose the leverage that makes the difference in the home. The first commandment with promise deals with respect for parents. It is imperative that you do not allow anything to make you less than what life has crowned you to be—a parent.

Sometimes when we have children at a very early age, we have a tendency not to see ourselves as parents. For whatever reasons we may assume a pseudo parental sphere whereby we might not even want our friends to hear us called "Mother" or "Daddy." But that is what we are, and we might as well get used to it.

I remember when my mother's hair started to turn gray. She absolutely hated it. For years she insisted on washing it out. Finally, when I started turning gray myself, I said to her, "Mother, don't you think that it looks strange for me to be your youngest child and have gray hair while yours is still black? Mother, you earned that gray hair. It is symbolic of your strength and determination to survive. Time has painted it on you at the expense of death. You have robbed the grave and denied death. In so doing, you have earned the trophy of silvery hair. It is yours. Wear it with dignity." She never dyed it again.

We can't all be young forever. Someone must be the parent so the other can be the child. There is a time in your life for frivolity and a time in your life for mentoring. This is the time that you contribute to your children. Give them a parent who is whole and healthy, and they will give you a child after its own kind. There is a line of distinction that comes from being a parent. It is crucial and necessary.

When Jacob was old and dying, he had the ability to bless his sons. The blessing of a father is a powerful thing. It will not be powerful if the man who is biologically your father has been so much your friend that his hand doesn't have the touch of a father.

The enemy comes to kill, steal and destroy. He desires to rob you of an important element in your life. The parent and the child have a unique bond between them. I will have but one mother and one father. I will have countless opportunities to have friends and whisper about silly, illicit off-color things if I so choose. But I have one chance at being a parent. I need that. So do my children.

I am their father. I will always love them and support them—and in an abstract sense, I am their friend. But they cannot be my friends. My friends see me in a completely different light. They are an outlet for me—a place of camaraderie without the responsibility of training.

I will have many friends. So will my children. But

we have only one chance to have this precious gift of parent and child. So I resist the temptation to be common and modern, to try foolishly to fit into a generation for which God did not design me. I will stand outside of their ring like a good coach and urge them on to victory. If I am not there to see them win, then I will be somewhere peering off a balcony in heaven, giving them a standing ovation because I know my place.

I am not just their friend. I am their father. What about you?

Discussion Questions

1. Everyone needs a friend. The author states: "Real friends cannot be bought, nor can you persuade anyone to love you. It just happens . . . It cannot be fully explained. It must be experienced."

   On the lines below, describe your closest friend and the impact that person has had on your life.

   _____

   _____

   _____

   _____

2. In this chapter we learned that when confronted with crisis, some parents wrongly try to find a level of fulfillment that was not meant to be achieved through their relationships with their children. T. D. Jakes said, "One of the most lethal side effects of this is the tendency to become too reliant on their children."

   Take time to think about your relationship with your children. Put a check next to each statement that describes a way you have related to your child. On the line below each checked statement, describe how you can make a more positive response to your child.

   ❏ I have shared negative facts about my ex-spouse with my children.

   _____

   _____

   ❏ I have treated my children like close friends and confidants, weighing them down with adult issues.

   _____

   _____

❑   I have vented my stress to my child.

_____

_____

❑   I have allowed my children to be disrespectful and dishonoring to me by words or attitudes.

_____

_____

3. Most experts believe that the major contributor to a child's confusion and dysfunction at the time of divorce is lack of adequate nurturing at the time the child needs it most.
    Think about the quality—and quantity—of nurturing that you are able to give to your family. On the lines below, list three ways that you can think of that would allow you to give additional nurturing to your children.

_____

_____

_____

_____

_____

_____

_____

_____

_____

_____

Shape Your Destiny Activity

"HOW I CAN RESPOND WHEN . . ."

Materials: Posterboard, marker, scissors, paper fastener.

Cut out a large 24-inch circle from the posterboard. Use a marker to divide the circle into eight pie-shaped sections. Label each section with the following words: Proud, Happy, Angry, Sad, Friendly, Loving, Spiteful, Forgiving. Cut out a 14-inch spinner arrow. Attach the spinner arrow to the center of the circle with a long paper fastener.

To play the game:

Each family member spins the pointer and role-plays a situation that portrays the word at which the spinner arrow stops. Encourage family members to role-play situations that have happened to them in their family relationships. Be sure they know that they are to role-play a positive way to respond to each situation—not necessarily in the way they may have responded in the past.

When each family member has had a chance to act out the best possible solution to the situation they were given, discuss other positive ways to deal with the kinds of situations these words suggest. Use the opportunity to encourage each member to take time to think about their actions before they respond to these situations when they come up in the future.

Do not allow family members to discuss the negative ways family members have responded in the past. Use the time to suggest and communicate new, improved positive ways to respond in the future.

Prayer

Father, thank You that Your Word is a guide to help me know how to be a good parent to my children. Thank You that Your Word helps my children know how to be obedient, respectful children. Help us to listen carefully to Your instructions and to follow Your Word as best we can.

To my children You have said, "My son, hear the instruction of your father, and do not forsake the law of your mother . . . for I give you good doctrine . . . Get wisdom! Get understanding! Do not forget, nor turn away from the words of my mouth . . . For they are life to those who find them, and health to all their flesh. Keep your heart with all diligence, for out of it spring the issues of life" (Prov. 1:8; 4:2, 5, 22–23, NKJV).

And to me You have said, "Oh, that [you] had such a heart in [you] that [you] would fear Me and always keep all My commandments, that it might be well with [you] and with [your] children forever" (Deut. 5:29, NKJV).

Father, my family and I commit our hearts and lives to You. We want You to be pleased with us. Father, this day, we say to You, "As for me and my house, we will serve the LORD" (Josh. 24:15). In Jesus' name, amen.

CHAPTER 8

Take Time
for Yourself

IT IS WISE AND THERAPEUTIC FOR YOU TO TAKE A LITTLE TIME FOR YOURSELF SO THAT IN THE PROCESS OF RAISING CHILDREN, YOU DO NOT BECOME ESTRANGED FROM YOURSELF. IT IS POSSIBLE TO LOSE SIGHT OF YOURSELF ASIDE FROM YOUR RESPONSIBILITIES. I AM GRACIOUSLY TELLING YOU THAT YOUR RESPONSIBILITIES CANNOT BECOME YOUR LIFE, BECAUSE SOON YOU WILL NOT BE NEEDED TO DO WHAT YOU DID LAST YEAR IN THE LIVES OF YOUR CHILDREN.

Come to Me, all you who labor and are heavy laden, and I will give you rest. Take My yoke upon you and learn from Me, for I am gentle and lowly in heart, and you will find rest for your souls. For My yoke is easy and My burden is light . . .

Do not remember the former things, nor consider the things of old. Behold, I will do a new thing, now it shall spring forth; shall you not know it? I will even make a road in the wilderness and rivers in the desert . . .

In You, O LORD, I put my trust; let me never be put to shame. Deliver me in Your righteousness, and cause me to escape; incline Your ear to me, and save me. Be my strong refuge, to which I may resort continually . . . O God, do not be far from me; O my God, make haste to help me! Let them be confounded and consumed who are adversaries of my life; let them be covered with reproach and dishonor who seek my hurt. But I will hope continually, and will praise You yet more and more. My mouth shall tell of Your righteousness and Your salvation all the day, for I do not know their limits. I will go in the strength of the Lord GOD.

—MATTHEW 11:28–30; ISAIAH 43:18–19;
PSALM 71:1–3, 12–16, NKJV

"How can I ever find time for all this?" If you are a single parent, you've asked that question. This chapter helps you to learn to manage your time so well that you will even have time for yourself!

Much can be said about time management in the life of a single parent. There seems not to be enough hours in the day nor energy in the body to respond to all of the needs. It can be physically draining and emotionally destructive to try to be everything. The simple truth is you cannot cover the absence of a companion. You can be sensitive to it and even help with it, but you cannot be two people.

You cannot effectively be everything to a child that both parents should be. It helps to know that even if you had help, that doesn't mean the help would be helpful. Many married people are raising their children alone simply because one of them doesn't support the child-rearing process. So do all you can, but realize the limitations of being one person cannot be ignored.

If you do ignore these limitations, you will find yourself overwhelmed, sitting on the floor eating cotton balls and talking out of your head. A nervous breakdown will not help you or your child. So pace yourself. We want you to make the long haul and not just the short sprint.

I think that the first enemy we must send home is guilt. Guilt makes most of us workaholics. We feel guilty when we rest. We feel that there is too much to be done. We feel that resting is not important weighed against the needs of others. But this is not being fair to you.

Remember Christ, who had only thirty-three years to accomplish His purpose and disciple grown men. He only used three of those years for ministry. Those must have been some power-packed years. It would be a bit stressful to be told that I had three years to impact the world so strongly that it would never be the same again; three years to so affect history that even agnostics and atheists would be discussing me for thousands of years after my life on earth. That would make me a bit stressed. How about you?

Now add to that demand the realization that He is God in a body, wrapped up in flesh. You know how He loved people. You would think that as God He would use every available moment—dismissing sleep and rest and relaxation—to accomplish His purpose. But that is not the case. He did not become an insomnia-ridden, sleepwalking computer that was driven by the needs of others to the degree that He offered Himself up on the altar of a demanding schedule rather than the cross. Over and over again we see that He rested!

Now if He was God and only had three years to minister, and yet He needed rest, how about you?

> And the apostles gathered themselves together unto Jesus, and told him all things, both what they had done, and what they had taught.
>
> And he said unto them, Come ye yourselves

apart into a desert place, and rest a while: for there were many coming and going, and they had no leisure so much as to eat. And they departed into a desert place by ship privately.

—MARK 6:30–32, KJV

Here Jesus teaches us that if you do not take time, you will get none. I feel awkward even teaching on this because it is an area that I myself struggle with even today. It is difficult to balance the demands of life against the human supply. I am learning that we just cannot do it all. As our situations change and our age changes, we can't even do as much of it as we once did.

The Bible says that the disciples were not even getting a chance to eat.

I learned how to take mealtime as a sabbath. I take no phone calls while I am eating. I learned to do that after getting on the phone in the middle of dinner and coming back two and one-half hours later after two or three overlapping phone calls to cold food and a dinner table where my children had gone to bed, tired of waiting on me to finish business. For me, one of my little sabbaths is mealtime.

You might take as a sabbath a long luxurious bath, complete with oils, scents and soft music. A little pampering is allowed to someone who gives so much. Remember, if you do not take it, you will not get it. No one is there with you to insist that you stop working but you. Children will not do it because they think you are indestructible. If you are going to keep up that image of being indestructible, you had better get a little rest.

Rest does not always have to be sleep. In fact, many times rest can be a deviation from the normal schedule. Rest can be having breakfast on the terrace away from everyone. A rest can be a weekend at a resort. If you do not take it, you will not get it.

It doesn't have to be expensive to be effective. Take a ride to the park with a book and a sandwich and spend a morning in peace. Get a relative to take the children out to the mall, the store or a movie. You will be glad you did. Most single parents only get a babysitter when there is work to be done. Take a break for you. Jesus took a rest, and He taught His disciples to rest.

David said, "He maketh me to lie down in green pastures" (Ps. 23:2, KJV). If you do not take a rest on your own, you might end up with a forced rest. I would rather go to the park on my own than end up in the hospital by force.

I am not trying to scare you but merely to warn you that it is wrong to neglect yourself to the point of becoming broken and wounded emotionally or physically. Yes, you are still there with the children, but you are grumpy and moody and depressed. They would enjoy you better if you had a time of refreshing.

The word *rest* literally means "to repose or to refresh." The next time you have to take a trip, why not take an extra day and go by train? Get a good book and relax. You might save some money, or greater still, you might relieve some stress and arrive more refreshed than you would have otherwise.

MAKING YOURSELF ACCESSIBLE WITHOUT ALWAYS BEING AVAILABLE

We are not talking about neglecting your responsibilities; we are talking about including yourself as a priority. Are you not important? Then there should be some provision for your renewal.

I know there are some who take it to extremes. But I believe that the majority of single parents are conscientious, hardworking people who have often forgotten how to relax and enjoy themselves outside of their role in the family. They have lost their sense of perspective and have ceased to be people. They are just single parents. That is all they are, and that is all they will allow themselves to be.

Many times that makes them cling to their children. They will not allow their children to grow up because they themselves are co-dependent. They need to be needed. They have put all of their reasons for living into children who are growing and weaning themselves continually.

Their expectations become unrealistic because subconsciously they almost expect their maturing children to put their lives—including friendships, careers and marriages—on hold and be there for them. When that doesn't happen, these parents do not feel loved. Sadly, they have failed to define love. They measure love by self-denial. It is a depressing place to end their lives.

They then become embittered against the very children they sacrificed to raise because these children are not "loving" them back in the way they want to be loved. It sounds dysfunctional, doesn't it? To a degree it is. It is not functioning the way it was designed. Your children were designed to leave you and cleave to someone else. They leave and cleave—that is the principle of the Scriptures.

> But from the beginning of the creation God made them male and female. For this cause shall a man leave his father and mother, and cleave to his wife; and they twain shall be one flesh: so then they are no more twain, but one flesh. What therefore God hath joined together, let not man put asunder.
>
> —MARK 10:6–9, KJV

Your children are assigned to you to raise. Parenthood was never meant to be ownership, just stewardship. That is why when Hannah prayed and asked God for a child, she told the Lord that she would give him back to God. That is what parenthood is all about—stewardship, caring for them and giving them back to God. You do not own them. They have their own minds and personalities. You help to train and direct their minds; you discipline and guide, but you will never be able to keep their minds.

It is wise and therapeutic for you to take a little time for yourself so that in the process of raising children, you do not become estranged from yourself. It is possible to lose sight of yourself aside from your responsibilities. I am graciously telling you that your responsibilities cannot become your life, because soon you will not be needed to do what you did last year in the lives of your children.

> Dear Dad,
>
> Thank you for holding me on your lap so I could see the game. Thank you for taking me to the carnival and buying me a hot dog. Oh, and thank you for the time you picked me up and carried me through the snow because I was so cold. You have been a great dad. I will never forget you.
>
> My wife, Suzy, and I were just talking about you. We were wondering how you are doing. Since we finished school and moved to Boston we don't get to see you much. But one day we are going to get in the car and just surprise you. Take care, Dad. I love you.
>
> Your son

Nice letter, eh? It is nice if you have prepared your

mind for the day that you will not be needed to do any of the things that were once your job description. If you did not, that same letter is a painful reminder that they have done what the Bible says they would do—leave and cleave.

Who are you aside from your children?

Women especially need to hear this because they are instinctively so maternal. If these women were married, good husbands would say to them, "Get out of the kitchen, leave that laundry sitting there, and stop working on the house. We are going out to dinner tonight." If you have no husband to pull you away, just pull yourself away. Every so often you need to say, "I deserve a break today."

Jesus shows us single parenting at its best. He is always accessible but not always available.

> And there arose a great storm of wind, and the waves beat into the ship, so that it was now full.
>
> And he was in the hinder part of the ship, asleep on a pillow: and they awake him, and say unto him, Master, carest thou not that we perish?
>
> And he arose, and rebuked the wind, and said unto the sea, Peace, be still. And the wind ceased, and there was a great calm. And he said unto them, Why are ye so fearful? How is it that ye have no faith?
>
> —MARK 4:37–40, KJV

I realize that I have taken theological liberties by referring to this text as an illustration of single parenting. While it may be a stretch theologically, it certainly is not one philosophically.

Philosophically, Jesus is the sole person to whom all twelve disciples look for guidance, provision and wisdom. He is with them all the time, training them and preparing them for a time when He will not be there. They are dependent on Him for most of their sustenance. He is riding in the boat with them. They are together. He is the one on whom they depend. In the midst of their journey, there arose a storm.

He was there on the ship, but the Bible says He was not available. In fact, He was in the hinder part of the ship. He was asleep when the storm broke out. He must have been asleep for a while because by the time they awoke Him, they thought they would perish in the storm.

Jesus did not neglect them; He was accessible, but He was not available for every little whimper that His children had. He knew that their faith needed to be exercised by resolving some dilemmas on their own.

Have you given your children the chance to act on what you have taught them? I know some people are neither available nor accessible. Their children are left continually to raise themselves. Others are so available that they never give their children the opportunity to learn any kind of responsibility.

How much responsibility can children handle? It varies from child to child, neighborhood to neighborhood. Responsibility will never develop if you are always available and they never learn to make rational choices on their own.

Jesus was close enough to help them but far enough away to allow them a chance to make choices. Notice the guilt trip they try to put on Him. "Carest thou not that we perish?" They in essence were saying, "If You really loved us, You would always be available."

Listen, friend. No one can always be available. Not you, not me, not Jesus. He is always accessible, but if He were always just hanging around, we would never learn to seek His face. Seeking Him is the privilege of prayer.

Can you see there are times that even your children need a break from you so they can exercise their teaching and training in a controlled atmosphere? Jesus was close enough to control it. He spoke to the storm and dismissed it, then He challenged them by asking, "Where is your faith?"

I learned as a child in the hills of West Virginia that if you run up and down those hills in the summer and stumble across a baby snake, be careful. Somewhere there is a mother snake around. She may not be available for you to see her. But you had better believe she is accessible.

Birds give their young space to learn and develop. Serpents, bears and other animals do, too. In fact, all of nature does it. Yet many single parents are afraid to take a night off and relax. They feel guilty.

Do not allow grandparents, parents or children to make you feel guilty just because you are resting a moment on the ship of parenting. After all, the family only visits the place where you live everyday.

Times are changing. Our parents lived a different life. Generally they had a different stress level. Many of us were raised in the country where the whole neighborhood helped to raise a child. In fact, we had neighborhoods filled with concerned (sometimes nosey) neighbors who would call our parents if we got into mischief. They would correct us, and we would have never thought of challenging any adult. Sure, we resented them, but we also respected them.

What a change from that to the distant cold relationship that exists between people who live near each other today. I do not call them neighbors, nor are they neighborhoods. They are holding tanks for colonies of people who are packed in, pressed down and overwhelmed by day-to-day challenges.

The neighborhood concept has in many cases turned into a septic tank! The attitude has moved from the village concept to an individualistic, self-promoting sort of posture. From the concrete jungles of the city apartments to the dank, dark, rodent-infested projects, there is a decadence of values and compassion. Even the elite suffer from a cold, distant attitude of indifference. I know what it is to live in better neighborhoods. Somehow the neighborhood is better, the conditions are certainly more opulent, but the concern is often sadly lacking.

All of these factors add to the lonely feeling of the single parent—living in an apartment building filled with people yet feeling quite alone. There is no solitude like the kind that arises from being alone in a crowd.

An apathy seems to permeate our society. The employer seems indifferent to the special challenges that single parenting brings. There is little compassion for events or phone calls from the school that require you to go pick up your child. The executive can send someone, but often you have no one to send to pick up your child.

Gradually the tides are turning. More and more large companies are providing day care and other amenities that are geared toward the needs of single parenting. You must find ways to stay abreast of anything that will make your life easier and your child rearing less complicated.

Many times we have a tendency to do things out of habit. We don't periodically investigate to see what services could be provided to make this job easier. Let's face it. If you are going to take any time for yourself, you must make a well-orchestrated effort. It must be planned and implemented in such a way to allow you to have the optimum care for your children without neglecting yourself.

Correct thy son, and he shall give thee rest; yea,
he shall give delight unto thy soul.

—PROVERBS 29:17, KJV

While we are discussing rest and replenishing, allow
me to interject a thought that might assist young parents
in ascertaining a stable place of rest in your own home.
Allow me to address it from one parent to the another.

Many parents get no rest because they fail to train
their children. I know—I have five children and a
demanding schedule. I know that children will be children, but I also realize that if they are trained, they do
not have to be destructive or selfish. You must teach
them to respect the rights of others.

The Bible says that a corrected son will give you
rest. The implication is that uncorrected children give
no rest. When children have not been trained, their
misbehavior becomes an albatross around your neck.
You cannot take them to visit other people. Others do
not want to keep them because they are a menace.

It is really not the children's fault. Training must
come early—very early if it going to be effective. I am
not speaking about child abuse, which is reprehensi-
ble and disgusting. But you must realize that child
neglect is just as bad. Neglecting the training of your
children makes them unmanageable. It affects their
ability to be trained in school or corrected in life.

Boundaries are healthy. When we understand that we
cannot do just anything, we also know that we are
loved—loved enough to be trained. Training is attention,
a wonderful attention for a child who will try the boundaries to see what he can get away with. If you do not
train him now, he will make your life miserable later.

A two-year-old sticking his tongue out at you and
saying no might seem cute. But wait until he is seven-
teen and cursing you like a mule skinner in August.

147

You will wonder why. You will think, *I loved you. I fed you. I washed your clothes and took care of you. Why don't you respect me?*

Realize that respect is not natural; it is a result of training. It is in the heart of a child to be rebellious. That doesn't mean that the child is not a good child—just untrained.

> A youngster's heart is filled with rebellion, but punishment will drive it out of him.
>
> —PROVERBS 22:15, TLB

Notice the phrase "drive it out of him." That implies that rebellion will not go out on its own. Anytime you drive something out, you force it out. Please understand that you can't wait until your child is almost ready for college to drive rebellion out of him. By that time he has become rigid in the boundaries that you have not established. It must come early if it is going to be effective.

Punishment doesn't always have to be physical to be effective. Your parenting style should be Spirit-led. That's right. Each child is different, and you and the Lord must commune to get the right combination for reaching that particular child. For some children a stern talk is effective. Others are unmoved by being scolded. Be sure that you are not using unnecessary force. If the child has a breaking of the will through a stern talk, corporal punishment might be unnecessary.

Caution: One thing that is never effective is flying into a fit of rage and venting your frustration on your children. It is unfair and destructive. That just teaches your children that they are worthless or it makes them violent. Either way, you will send them into society maimed at the hands of a butcher parent who failed to use wisdom. Calm down. Never, never punish your child while you are in a rage. This leads to child abuse. Child abuse is illegal and immoral. What's more, it is not effective.

You cannot punish them for everything they do wrong. But be careful that you are not so full of grace that they become like the men in Jude who turned the grace of God into lasciviousness. The term *lasciviousness* means "to have unrestrained actions." No boundaries exist. The walls are down and anything goes. They need boundaries. Boundaries are healthy and effective.

They need a bedtime. No, they shouldn't be up all night and then be expected to do well in school. If you are lonely, invite a friend over and have your children go to bed. They are children, and they need boundaries.

Who would want a house without walls? Walls give us a feeling of safety and protection. No one wants to live in a carport with all sides exposed; you can go in or out at will. To raise your children without discipline is to make them a carport. They are lascivious. They have no boundaries, and they are a city without walls. No wonder you have no time. They stay up late at night then sleep late in the morning.

There is no structure. Yet your life is structured. When you have a structured life, your children must have a structured life. Otherwise their lack of discipline will make you late for work, ruin your relationships with friends and admirers and worse, rob you of the rest you need to continue.

Now if we manage to clear a little time, the question is, What should we do with that time? For some, rest is coming home at night, turning on some soft music and slipping into a hot tub of bubbly water. If this is you, being able to rest your mind, allowing the tingling feeling of hot water to massage the stress out of your body, epitomizes luxury that is tailored for the soul.

Others may choose to read a book or just close their eyes and let music fill the moment.

This type of tranquillity need not be expensive or elongated. It may be a brief interlude of refreshing. All of us need a sabbath in our lives, a sabbath that does not lend itself to accountability or responsibility. In it we answer to no one. This is a moment that is completely our own.

For some, tranquillity is defined as a day or two for leaving at the crack of dawn with a few rods and reels, listening to the sounds of nature as it yawns and wakes up in the morning. A place is chosen somewhere that is surrounded by palatial mountains and cool streams of waters where a deep and total sublimity hides. Yes, there is a place of seclusion deeply submerged in the woods where dewdrops of tranquillity are so serene that problems dissipate in the fragrance of that moment.

In this place whether or not you catch any fish is not the issue. It is a matter of the mindless wanderings and the escapades of frivolous thought as you are renewed alone in the presence of the Lord. It doesn't matter how you design the rest. It just matters that you have it.

One of the definitions listed in the dictionary for *weariness* is, "to have your sense of pleasure exhausted." That is to say that when you are weary, you have no sense of pleasure. We enjoy things less when we are tired. We enjoy life less, relationships less, people less and even our children less.

If you don't get rest, you become so lethargic and indifferent that you gain little pleasure from your own life. It will leave you laughing in a crowd but unhappy in your heart. You need some rest. No, you cannot retire, but you can take mini-vacations.

Many times our actions teach people that we are not important. We keep serving ourselves up to everyone with whom we are associated. They gradually learn from our actions that we have no needs. That is not true; it is an illusion. Even the most giving person has needs.

If we condition our children to believe that we have no needs, that absolutely everything is about their needs and no one else is important, then we are teaching them to be self-centered. So take a little time for yourself. When you are healed and whole, you can give more to them without feeling as though the pleasure has gone out of your life.

I can almost hear some loving mother saying, "Oh, you don't understand that my children are my joy." Yes, I do. I know that they fulfill a need in your life. I also understand that they do not fulfill every need in your life. As you go and as you grow there are other needs that all of us have, like the need to be affirmed, the need to be appreciated, the need to recuperate.

Finally, I understand that all too often single parents make their children their whole life. Then when the child grows increasingly independent, they feel betrayed. Do not start that. Love them, nurture them and support them, but take a little time for yourself.

I want to move on, but before I do, please allow me to speak to that area in you that hides behind your responsibilities. Allow me to minister to that area in your heart that appreciates the values and gifts in others without recognizing your own. It is so important that you bring balance in your heart. I am praying for you that you share your life with your children. But also share some of that life with yourself. If your children really love you, and I am sure they do, they will be glad to see you happy.

Also, stop hiding behind the business. I am praying

that you master a schedule that is trying to master you. I want you to realize that God cares for your every need. He has given you a life. It is your life to enjoy as you serve Him. What you do with that life is largely a result of your decisions. Please include yourself in your plans. Take a night off and go for a walk by the river and make yourself sit on the banks and relax. It doesn't take long, but it is so important.

> He maketh me to lie down in green pastures: he leadeth me beside the still waters. He restoreth my soul.
> —PSALM 23:2–3, KJV

David says God made him lie down. That literally means that God made him "recline like a recumbent animal." It sounds good. The end result is, "He restoreth my soul."

I have concern about the process of being made to lie down. As I told you earlier, we don't want to be made to lie down. Night comes through afflictions. When I was small, my brother used to wrestle me to the floor and hold me down. It is much better to lie down on your own.

If you are tired and exhausted in such a way that sleep does not relieve it, if you go to bed tired and wake up tired, you must understand that chances are you are not in need of sleep alone. You are in need of rest.

Sometimes rest is change. Sometimes rest is reclining and renewing your mind. Stop thinking so much, thinking the same thoughts day after day. Just rest. Rest in the Lord. It is His good pleasure to give you whatever you need. Rest in the fact that God is with you. This is the day that the Lord has made. He made it, but you are the one who must rejoice in what He has made and be glad in it.

Jesus says, "I will give you rest." In the New Testament He says, "I will give it to you." In the Old Testament David says, "He makes me lie down." Which would you prefer—to be given rest or to be made to lie down? Make the right choice while you still can. If I were you, I would choose to accept the rest that is given rather than finding myself forced into a crouched position like an animal forced to sit. Come on, take a little time for yourself and just rest. Rest in Him.

Perhaps you have gotten so busy that you can't find rest. You can't find rest at home or at work. Perhaps you can't find rest in church. There are times you can't find rest in sleep. God says if you would come to Him rather than trying to be Him, the very thing that you cannot find apart from Him is the thing that He will give you.

My friend, you have given so much to others, but today, there is something that God wants to give you. He will give you rest.

> Come unto me, all ye that labour and are heavy laden, and I will give you rest.
>
> —MATTHEW 11:28, KJV

Discussion Questions

1. Have you felt like "sitting on the floor eating cotton balls and talking out of your head" because of all the demands upon your time as a single parent? The author teaches us that time management is one of the best tools we can learn to use. On the lines provided below, outline a typical day—including housework and all.

    6:00 A.M.–9:00 A.M.

    _____

    _____

    9:00 A.M.–Noon

    _____

    _____

    Noon–3:00 P.M.

    _____

    _____

    3:00 P.M.–8:00 P.M.

    _____

    _____

    8:00 P.M.–Midnight

    _____

    _____

2. The author talks about the importance of learning to take little "sabbaths"—moments of time for yourself or for quality time with your family. Review your typical day above. Determine where you can insert little "sabbaths" into your schedule—and determine to do so. Specify what you will do during these private moments.

Sabbath 1:

_____

Sabbath 2:

_____

Sabbath 3:

_____

Sabbath 4:

_____

Sabbath 5:

_____

3. It is very easy to "use" a busy schedule to keep yourself from taking necessary time to reflect on your life and deal with negative roots that need to turned into positive steppingstones to wholeness. What negative roots do you need to deal with yet?

_____

_____

_____

4. Schedule in a specific time and way to deal with these roots. Perhaps you need the counsel of a Christian mentor. Maybe you just need to give yourself time to think about these roots and determine to make an adjustment. On the lines below tell how you will do this.

_____

_____

_____

Shape Your Destiny Activity

FAMILY MEMBER "SABBATHS"

Materials: Paper, pencils.

Gather each family member in a circle. Explain that today you are going to discuss ways to help all family members experience a period of time when they have the opportunity to do something they really enjoy.

Spend some time letting each family member answer this question: "If you could choose a really fun activity that you would like to do and that our entire family could share with you (without spending a lot of money), what would it be?" Talk about the suggestions, and discuss alternatives to activities that cost a lot of money or involve a lot of advance preparation.

Then allow each family member to write down on paper the activity that member chooses to do. Take time to add any necessary details, such as materials needed, pertinent information and how to involve the whole family. When the entire family has agreed on the choices made by each family member, write on a calendar the day that each family member will be able to get the entire family together to participate in the activity. (Note: These can be a simple as taking a field trip to a nearby lake to swim or going to the park for a hot dog roast.)

Be sure to schedule the activities over a period of time so that they are not all taking place in one month. When the first round of activities has been completed, gather the family back together to plan another group of family outings.

Prayer

Father, I pray that You will forgive me for letting the busyness of our family's life prevent my children and I from taking little "sabbaths" to refresh our spirits and renew our souls. Teach us to take care of ourselves. Help me to realize that I don't have to do everything—that I don't have to be two parents to my children. Help me to see the importance of people and relationships over stuff and work that needs to be done.

Father, at times a great storm has come into my life, and the waves have beaten against my life until I thought I would sink. When those storms come, help me to remember that You will rebuke the wind, and will say to the sea, "Peace, be still." Give me the faith to trust You and not to fear.

Teach me—and my children—that You "maketh me to lie down in green pastures: [You] leadeth me beside the still waters. [You] restoreth my soul" (Ps. 23:2–3, KJV).

Help us to remember that "length of days and long life and peace" will be added to our family (Prov. 3:2, NKJV). I know that "the LORD will be [our] confidence" (Prov. 3:26, NKJV). In Jesus' name, amen.

CHAPTER 9

Will You Marry My Children, Too?

I DO NOT WANT YOUR DREAM TO TURN INTO A NIGHTMARE. SPECIAL CONSIDERATIONS MUST BE CONFRONTED WHEN YOU BRING CHILDREN INTO A MARRIAGE. IF THIS IS THE RIGHT MATE, IT CAN BE AN ANSWER TO PRAYER. IF THIS IS NOT, IT WILL BE A BITTER PILL WITH A LONG AFTERTASTE . . . BEFORE YOU GIGGLE AND SNICKER AND PROMISE YOUR FUTURE AWAY, ALWAYS, BUT ALWAYS, ASK HIM, "YES, BUT WILL YOU MARRY MY CHILDREN?"

Now it shall come to pass, if you diligently obey the voice of the LORD your God, to observe carefully all His commandments which I command you today, that the LORD your God will set you high above all nations of the earth. And all these blessings shall come upon you and overtake you, because you obey the voice of the LORD your God:

Blessed shall you be in the city, and blessed shall you be in the country.

Blessed shall be the fruit of your body, the produce of your ground and the increase of your herds, the increase of your cattle and the offspring of your flocks.

Blessed shall be your basket and your kneading bowl.

Blessed shall you be when you come in, and blessed shall you be when you go out . . .

If you do not oppress the stranger, the fatherless, and the widow . . . then I will cause you to dwell in this place, in the land that I gave to your fathers forever and ever.

—DEUTERONOMY 28:1–6, NKJV;
JEREMIAH 7:6–7, NKJV

Before you take that walk up the altar, be sure there is room in the aisle—and in your marriage partner's life—for both you and your children. In this chapter you will learn the principles to make that new marriage a haven of safety for you and your children.

Lovely music fills the chapel. The air is laced with the fragrance of flesh flowers. Music wafts upward in the room from an organ gently played in the morning light. There is the quiet murmuring of old friends who have not seen each other for a while. Gentlemen are looking starchily pressed. Ladies are arrayed in the soft colors of spring flowers. Romance reverberates in the room, titillating the senses like a fine wine in a chilled glass.

It is the moment that this couple has longed for. It is the time that they demonstrate publicly what they have felt privately. Their hearts now display what has been known between them for a while. They are to be married.

This is the rich fulfillment of some little girl's dream. From the days of Barbie and Ken, she has had a dream of chivalry and gallantry that has been illuminated in the magnitude of a moment. Neither the finest shadows nor eyeliners could decorate her eyes more beautifully than the gleam of expectation that twinkles like stars shimmering in the night. She is immersed in the sense of a love long past due.

In the distance is heard the sound of clinking glass and pots being stirred as the caterer prepares his culinary delights. This is the day! Somewhere in her mind she presses back a thought. A brief wrinkle breaks out on her forehead. She wonders, Will it work? Can he accept my children? I know he loves me, but can he love my three-year-old?

It would be different if her children were grown and gone. But no, these are children who need the firm hand of a loving father. Not just the firm hand of a father, but the firm hand of a loving father.

The bridesmaids have already started the procession. The mothers of the bride and groom have been seated, the solo has been sung. The bride is waiting in the wings, hands trembling, flowers shaking. This is the moment. Little rose petals are being dropped out of the hands of someone whose small fingers remind her of her own child.

The groom is standing by the preacher. He is starched and neat. He has never looked more gallant. He looks as if he could sweep her away with him without further adieu.

But, whoa. This is not that simple, is it? When they pull away from the wedding, there will be more than just the couple in the car. He cannot just whisk her off and leave her child. Will his warmth extend beyond the fragrance of her cologne and reach around and embrace the child that is her own? Is there passion in his eyes for the child that he has taken?

Perhaps we should alter the ceremony just a tad. Perhaps we should have the bride walk to the altar with her children. Yes, when she walks up the aisle she should have her children beside her. They are getting married, too. Because when he marries her, he cannot fail to marry her children.

How can you love me and not love what is my own flesh? This question needs to be addressed long before the processional of a wedding ceremony. Perhaps we should talk about single parents who are about to be married again.

Whether or not to marry is always a tough decision. It is increasingly tough if you are trying to choose a mate for you and a companion for your children. This is true even if you are a man raising your children alone. Just because she promises to be a wonderful wife, a great cook, a progressive businesswoman and an ardent lover, that still doesn't mean that she is ready to be a great mother. You must have a standard—"To marry me is to marry my circumstances and my children."

As a pastor I have often wanted to change the ceremony to say, "Do you take this woman and her children to be your lawfully wedded family?" That is the question that we need to hear, and "I do," too.

I have seen too many couples who fused together as if they had been welded by God Himself, but they had not discussed the children. They did not discuss their faith or how they may differ in child-rearing ideas. These differences will not show up in the marital bed of bliss. But oh, my God, the morning after!

What happens when he sends your child to bed without dinner? That is not necessarily a problem if you both agree on this method of discipline. But what if you see it as abusive and he sees it as effective? Suddenly your motherly instincts rise up and do war with your feminine attraction.

You should have read the fine print before you signed the contract. Didn't you discuss these issues?

Did you discuss what time you think children should go to bed? Did you notice whether he held the baby as tightly as he held you?

If you are a man, did you check to see if she minded giving herself to them? Is she the kind of girl who can run to the PTA meeting after work without complaining? Is she genuinely interested in your children or just in you? What sense of well-being do the children feel? They are very sensitive and can easily discern when someone loves them or not. Isn't it terrible to force them to go from a broken home to an abusive one?

They have no one to trust except the parent with whom they are bonded. Have you protected them? Or are you just so glad to have a friend that you have offered up on the altar the security and happiness of your children?

The real issue is, do you believe that God would send someone to you who didn't fit into and conform with your situation? Didn't God know you had children? Would He really send you someone who didn't like children? Of course not. So who is this who holds your hand yet pinches your child?

I just do not want your dream to turn into a nightmare. Special considerations must be confronted when you bring children into a marriage. If this is the right mate, it can be an answer to prayer. If this is not, it will be a bitter pill with a long aftertaste.

So let's hit a rewind button on this wonderful wedding and examine some questions and issues that must be picked out before we pick out caterers and florist. Let's make sure your soon-to-be great lover is also a soon-to-be great father. Let's be sure that the girl who has that wonderful 38-26-38 figure is also able to mix oatmeal, do homework and wash dark stains out of little Johnny's shirts. Have you considered reality or just romance?

Will You Marry My Children, Too?

I want to give you a little quiz that will help you to determine some issues that need to be resolved in advance. Depending on your answers to these questions you should or should not proceed with this course of action. I hope you can answer them honestly because your children's lives, as well as your own, depend on the validity of your answers to these issues.

The following are just a few questions that will help relieve future disappointment:

- Are you comfortable enough to share the government and discipline of your children with your intended spouse? Or are you going to get halfway down the road and start saying, "Wait a minute, that is my child"?

- Do you agree on discipline as well as privileges?

- Who will administer the punishment and what kind of punishment will that be?

- Have you discussed child-rearing techniques with your intended?

- Do you have the same value systems?

- Is college for the children a priority to both of you?

- What age do you think is a good age for your child to begin to date?

- Can you relax when your children and your intended are alone together?

- When your intended takes your child out alone, does it work out well? Or does the child seem distant and forced?

BONDING WITH THE CHILDREN

Do you sense that there has been enough time shared between your intended and your children to cause a bonding? I caution you that bonding cannot be commanded. You cannot force them to bond. Bonding is a matter to bathe in prayer.

I know that we can fuse two plants together, but only God could make them bond. It has to happen naturally. If it is not happening, please, please wait. Do not marry someone and then think you will change him or her later. That generally doesn't work, and besides, it isn't fair—especially if your intended was honest with you and told you in advance about his or her weaknesses. You knew from the beginning when you walked down the aisle or waited at the altar you were giving your consent and affirmation to what you knew about them!

When you allow your intended and your children time to bond, it is important that the bonding is not just happening when you are around. Many times you will try so hard to make it work that you will get in the way. If it is real, it should work when you are not around to force it. They have to bond. You are hopefully already bonded to the children. But if your intended is going to be there in the house, he or she must be bonded with your children also, or you will always be distraught about their actions and attitudes toward your children.

RESPECTING YOUR CHILDREN IN THE PROCESS

Respect your children enough to allow them to speak to you about your intended without trying to manipulate their opinion. Yes, you can overpower them into silence. You may intimidate them into silence, but you know as well as I do that opinions don't go away because of pressure or fear of scorn; they just hide.

I think that my creativity as a man is a direct result of being raised by a mother who respected my opinion. By doing that, she taught me to respect my own ideas. What a blessing it has been in my adult life to have a healthy ability to evaluate things and make decisions without losing confidence in my own opinion.

Feelings are significant. They help us, just as instincts help the animal to survive in the jungle. So allow them to speak. They may change their opinion. We all do that, but please allow them to express their opinion in a respectful way.

Have you ever had someone try to make you like something or someone that you did not like? You might smile, but in your heart you are still leery. Are your children comfortable with your choice? I know it is your business, but they have to live with your choice also.

It is so vulnerable to be a child. You have to live with the policy, but you are not allowed to vote! Therefore, it is not good to try to force them to love someone.

Also you must make sure that your intended respects your children. You must realize that our perceptions are often biased by our positions. Many times we think that a person is great based on their treatment of us. What we must realize is that they may not treat our children the same way that they treat us.

CONCERNS FOR YOUR CHILDREN

I have seen many parents dismiss their children's objections as simple childishness. Indeed they may be. But it is worth your while to examine the issue with objectivity. Because the truth of the matter is, we always like or dislike people on the basis of how they treat us.

I must caution you to watch also for those who

would come and be too intimate with your children. Do they spend more time with your children than with you? Does their personality seem unusually childish or bashful? Are they uncomfortable in adult settings but very comfortable with children? Have you noticed them going out of their way to be in intimate situations with your children—bathing them, massaging them?

None of these things by themselves are significant, but if they all seem present, you might need to investigate a little deeper. Is the newly introduced parent always trying to be alone with a child who doesn't want to go with him or her? Has your child waxed sullen, stopped eating or become withdrawn or depressed?

I hate even bringing this up. It is so unthinkable. You, like myself, probably think that it is too far-fetched to even mention it. It only happens on television. It is trapped on the six o'clock news. No, the truth is, child abuse of the sexual nature has reached epidemic proportions in this country. The church had better start talking about these issues, because they are happening.

Some of you know what it is like to be improperly handled or fondled by an adult when you were a child. When that is the case, you can easily become paranoid and overly sensitive. It is easy for you to think the worst because this kind of brokenness seems so real to you, but balance yourself. Please do not be suspicious of everyone who touches your child. I encourage you not to accuse someone without evidence. You must be wise.

On the other hand, please do not think that it does not happen, especially with stepfathers and stepmothers who do not always have a wholesome parental attitude for the child. Most stepmothers and stepfathers are marvelous heroes who gallantly mend with love and affection the broken homes and hearts of those who have been victimized. They are men and women of excellence whose attitudes should be commended.

In those terrible cases in which a person is still wrestling with that kind of character flaw, we must be able to minister to you in a preventive attempt at salvaging the quality of your life and your child's.

I know you say it cannot happen in the church. It can happen anywhere. The church draws hurting people. We attract people who have scars that need to be healed. God does heal. He is able to heal them from their past hurts. Please wait until the healing is over before you bring them into a situation that may endanger the quality of your life.

I bleed for the fathers and mothers who have stepped into the nightmare of a companion who abuses their child—sexually, physically or emotionally. I bleed even more for the child.

The tragedy occurs when the child becomes isolated with the problem because a parent does not believe his report. Children do lie. However, thousands of children in this country are not lying. They are the silent screamers who cry out in the night to ears that will not listen.

Be sure you are not unreachable and unrealistic just because you have been lonely and finally found someone. Make sure that someone is interested in you and then has a wholesome affection for the children. You must guard your children. Your happiness and fulfillment are being threatened seriously if night doors are creaking and morning finds little ones weeping. Silent tears of shame are imprisoned behind wide-eyed children who have something that needs to be said but no one they trust to say it to.

The majority of men and women in this world would never think of abusing a child in any way. Yet a degree of caution must be taken. Abuse and neglect are painful realities. I have counseled the cold remains of decomposed hearts that grew up in homes where these issues were not confronted. They are cold, rigor-mortis-ridden adults who are still struggling with childhood issues.

While we fight to heal them, I think it is wise to put some effort into prevention. I would rather use my ministry to prevent these abuses than to have to come along later and try to put salve on the hearts of children who have become bitter against life because Mom or Dad married someone who wasn't married to them.

In essence, children in this situation feel as if they have lost both parents. They lost the one they had to the one they didn't even know. It doesn't have to be that way if the single parent will regard the child in the process of the plan. They will respect you, you will respect yourself and a tragedy can be prevented before it begins.

So as you stand there in your tuxedo or gown, whichever the case may be, beneath the fragrance of roses and tinkling sound of crystal, understand that when the wedding day ends, there is the rest of the week with which to contend. It will be filled with the sounds of bicycles and Nintendo games. Look deeply into the eyes of your intended. Look for the calm peace of a new father or mother who fits snugly into the rest of your children's lives. Many women and men enjoy the spouse *and* the children. Find one.

The bonding between children and the stepparent is significant. It is as essential as the air we breathe. The stepparent cannot see them as simply your children. They have to see them as a commitment to produce excellence. I am glad for those who choose to enter into the ring of marriage. It is wonderful for those who are so inclined. Yet the older we get, the less willing we are to endure changes. Like the old oak tree, the branches become less flexible with age.

Be sure that this is what you want. If it is, congratulations are in order. Marriage is a wonderful thing. But when you kneel on one knee and ask that all important question, remember to bow your head in deepest sincerity and fix your eyes on hers. Question her honestly and candidly, "You are interested in marrying me, but will you marry my children?"

If you are the silky satin hand that is being held by the man you always wanted to come into your life, before you giggle and snicker and promise your future away, always, but always, ask him, "Yes, but will you marry my children?"

Discussion Questions

1. Whether or not to marry always is a tough decision. This chapter included a short quiz to help us make a wise decision about getting married again. Let's take that quiz now. Answer each question on the line below the question.

    Are you comfortable enough to share the government and discipline of your children with your intended spouse? Or are you going to get halfway down the road and start saying, "Wait a minute, that is my child"?

    _____

    Do you agree on discipline as well as privileges?

    _____

    Who will administer the punishment, and what kind of punishment will that be?

    _____

    Have you discussed child-rearing techniques with your intended?

    _____

    Do you have the same value systems?

    _____

    _____

    Is college for the children a priority to both of you?

    _____

    What age do you think is a good age for your child to begin to date?

    _____

    _____

Can you relax when your children and your intended are alone together?

_____

When your intended takes your child out alone, does it work out well? Or does the child seem distant and forced?

_____

2. List the characteristics that you would like your husband (or wife) to have in order to be compatible with you as a marriage partner.

_____

_____

3. Now list the characteristics that you would like your husband (or wife) to have in order to be a wonderful stepparent for your children.

_____

_____

_____

Shape Your Destiny Activity

FLOUR AND SALT CLAY FAMILY IMAGES

Materials: Flour, salt, water, food coloring, plastic containers (or plastic bags), waxed paper, aluminum foil, cleanup supplies, Destiny Tree (from chapter one).

Optional materials: Paint, paint brushes, smocks (or old T-shirts).

Prepare clay prior to this activity by using the following recipe: 4 cups flour, 1 cup salt, 1½ cups water. Mix flour and salt. Add water. Knead exactly as you would bread or clay. The more you knead, the better the texture. Store in closed containers or plastic bags. Clay may be colored with food coloring if desired.

During this activity, give each family member a piece of waxed paper to work on and a piece of aluminum foil for the finished project.

Advise the family members that you would like each of them to make a self-image, showing how they think they look. It should represent not only their clothes, hair and so on, but also how they feel and their expressions. Allow each family member to explain their image to the rest of the family.

These images may be baked in an oven at 350 degrees until golden brown. Spray with a fine mist of water before baking. If desired, each family member can paint his or her image. When all the clay figures are completed, hang them from the "Destiny Tree" that your family made during the family activity for chapter one.

Prayer

For your prayer today, write a prayer on the lines below that expresses your heart's cry for a mate who would be a wonderful spouse and parent in your home. Include your commitment to wait for a mate who you know—beyond any doubt—is God's choice for you.

_____

_____

_____

_____

_____

_____

_____

_____

_____

_____

CHAPTER 10

Ghost Parents

CHILDREN DON'T CARE MUCH ABOUT BUDGETS. THEY DO NOT UNDERSTAND DEADLINES OR INVENTORIES, STOCK EXCHANGES OR BONDS. THEY JUST WANT YOU. ISN'T THAT WHY WE LOVE THEM SO, BECAUSE OF THE PURITY OF THEIR LOVE? THEY LOVE US UNCONDITIONALLY. PERHAPS IN SOME WAYS THEY HAVE SPOILED US. THEY HAVE ALLOWED MANY TO BE REMISS IN THEIR DUTIES AND LOVED THEM ANYWAY.

At the same time came the disciples unto Jesus, saying, Who is the greatest in the kingdom of heaven? And Jesus called a little child unto him, and set him in the midst of them, and said, Verily I say unto you, except ye be converted, and become as little children, ye shall not enter into the kingdom of heaven. Whosoever therefore shall humble himself as this little child, the same is greatest in the kingdom of heaven.

And whoso shall receive one such little child in my name receiveth me. But whoso shall offend one of these little ones which believe in me, it were better for him that a millstone were hanged about his neck, and that he were drowned in the depth of the sea.

—MATTHEW 18:1–6, KJV

This chapter is focused on parents—single or married—
who contribute little or no emotional support and quality
or quantity time to their children.

I call some parents ghost parents because they
haunt the loved ones who live in the house. Yes, I
guess they are real, but you would never know it.
These are the ones who leave all the real responsibility
of raising the children to their spouse while they blow
in, blow up and blow out. They are ghosts indeed. The
creaking of rusted promises fills the air with the omi-
nous sound of despairing expectations—expectations
that have fermented in the kettles of frustration waiting on the promises to be fulfilled.

Many ghost parents are male, but some are female.
Gender doesn't always guarantee commitment. These
are not divorced or separated couples. These are not single parents. They are married but distracted. Some are
distracted by money, others by affairs. Some are distracted by a mentality that sees child rearing as being
beneath them. These wallflowers hear the music of parenthood but never dance. They sway as if they would,
but seldom do they go beyond a taunting, teasing

promise that leaves both the other parent and the child in a constant state of frustration.

You don't have to be single to be a single parent. Many are legally and physically married, but when it comes to the ministry of child rearing, one of them doesn't seem to want to participate. Sadly, the children are left with a disenchanted feeling as they realize the disappointment of this ghost parent not caring about their lives.

I can remember times when this was a very sexist issue. You seldom heard of a mother who didn't become involved in the lives of her children. Today that is not always the case. Many women have traded their aprons and oatmeal for briefcases and PCs.

I certainly do not criticize successful women. I just point out that workaholics generally used to be men, partially because years ago women were not well-received in most work settings. The ridiculous ideology then was that the woman's place was in the home. I know, I said it was ridiculous. I say so because the Scriptures describe the virtuous woman in Proverbs 31 to be both domestically and economically endowed. She was a businesswoman.

Nevertheless, women who enter into certain arenas of stress face some severe hardships today. In days gone by, the circumstances were much different. Men left their wives little notes like, "I will be late coming home from work." "I can't make it to the family outing because of . . . " Men were calling and saying, "I can't make Johnny's football game. Will you go for me? I have go to work." Now women are being bogged down with that kind of responsibility.

If both parents work, many couples compromise and share the responsibilities at home. Yet there are some cases in which one partner becomes so engrossed in becoming successful that the rearing of the children is left to the other parent. Many reasons may contribute to this attitude—everything from being a workaholic to false stereotypes of "macho-ism."

Many times the liberated woman of this generation finds it difficult to compete with her female competition who have given up the apron for the briefcase, not to mention men who are sometimes cynical and adversarial regarding her ascent to success. This high-stress, highly competitive work arena becomes engrossing, and the child who didn't ask to be born is tossed around like old luggage. Many times the child who lives with his two biological parents spends an inordinate amount of time home alone!

Are there easy solutions? Not really. Left unattended, this situation becomes a growing source of frustration for the one parent who constantly has to explain why the other never becomes involved. It becomes an endless job for the parent who, regardless of gender, needs a break.

What is shocking is the fact that the parent is married and yet is still a single parent. They tackle all the tough issues from the child asking questions such as "Can I go out this evening?" to the difficult school problems and gang violence. The other parent seems almost in denial that they are a part of the team. They think their responsibility ends with the provision of money. Generally guilt drives them to spending an incredible amount of money as compensation for their absentee parenthood.

Am I stepping on some toes? Good! We are in a battle to save the seed. It takes both parents whenever possible to achieve our goal. Tragically, children generally yearn more for the attention of the absent parent than they do for the one who did their job. It can be frustrating for the parent who has stood by like Old Faithful to hear the child make over the slightest attention from the other parent who is virtually irresponsible when it comes to rearing children. There are some things you need to understand.

We never crave what we were fed. We crave what we were not given. I mean that children always long for the attention from the parent who was uninvolved, not the one who was involved. They long for and often overreact to any attention from the absentee parent. If you do not understand that, you will misunderstand it and feel hurt. The child longs for the missing link, not the present one.

This is not an indictment against the one who was there. It is a glaring indictment against the one who wasn't. It openly and emphatically displays how desperately your child wants that attention and affection.

I can relate to this issue so well because in my own life one parent was by far more involved with my early rearing than the other. In my case it was my mother who was always right there for us. She literally seemed bionic. She cooked, cleaned, sewed, handled school problems, planted gardens and more. It was my mother who showed up at band concerts and football games, who broke up fights and explained the birds and the bees.

I realize in retrospect that my father, who was a marvelous man, was busy trying to maneuver our family into economic stability. That was no easy feat for a black man in the fifties and sixties. He worked around the clock for peanuts. I understand why now. At the time, I just missed his affirmation. I thought he didn't want to be bothered. He had allowed my mother to assume areas that he should have maintained. He had become a ghost parent.

He was there in spirit, but his flesh was long gone. He was absent from the football games and the concerts. Eventually I became accustomed to his faintly fading image disappearing through the door, always rushing out to fix something somewhere else—anywhere else but home. As the door slammed, the house shook, the floor vibrated and I . . . well, I just wondered what it would be like to go fishing or boating or anything that all the other children seemed to do with their dads.

He was a ghost parent to me. What was worse, I became a ghost child. I suppose that is what it is when grown-ups walk past you and pat your head as if you were a collie dog and grunt something to you that you didn't even understand. My, what a struggle it was for them to survive.

My dad is dead now. I respect him more in death than I understood him in life. I guess it is because now I have the responsibilities and the needs and the bills. I try, and I want you to try also, to just remember that one of the greatest provisions possible is your attention. Just sprinkle it anywhere like salt. It will enhance the flavor of the man inside the boy or the woman inside the girl.

Children don't care much about budgets. They do not understand deadlines or inventories, stock exchanges or bonds. They just want you. Isn't that why we love them so, because of the purity of their love? They love us unconditionally. Perhaps in some ways they have spoiled us. They have allowed many to be remiss in their duties and loved them anyway.

Beware, however, because later that bug may fly back and bite you when you least expect it. Later when your life slows down, you will want—no, need—their attention. The tragedy becomes more pronounced when your bones are stiff and your eyes feeble. Remember, where there is no deposit, there is little hope of a great withdrawal.

Ghost parents think that what the other parent does makes up for or in some way compensates for what they themselves have not done. They do not know that they are missed from the table, missed from the recital or missed from the argument over the car keys. The memories that will become the conversation pieces of a lifetime are not being formed because they have shared their lives with everyone except the ones who loved them the most.

I will be honest and say it is difficult for those of us who had ghost parents not to become one. Periodically someone has to rattle some chains to keep us from evaporating into our jobs, ministries or responsibilities. If you are married to a ghost, don't let him live and die and miss his children. Wake him up; wake her up.

Life means nothing without someone with whom to share it. What good is a rose garden without an eye to behold it? When you have attained the all-consuming success that you seek, will it matter? Will it matter if your children have become so distant that they struggle to make conversation with someone they are related to but cannot relate to?

Ghost parents are phantoms, male and female, black and white, educated and illiterate. They stalk the hearts of confused children who wonder why they have not seen more than a brief shadow of a parent who keeps disappearing from view. These bicycle-bringing, TV-dinner-providing moms and dads are as frigid as an ice cream cone. They are chilled by the cold blister of facts and figures, of goals and ambitions that lack purpose and meaning.

I bleed for all of the spouses of ghost parents. These

are the ones who clamor for excuses to explain to the children without hurting them why they should not expect support right now. These are the parents who lie down in the bed with a thud and pull their weary feet beneath the covers with someone—someone whose interest has begun just as sleep has gripped the heart of the other who has spent all her strength trying to cover for him.

Rest is lost in fitful sleep—the kind of sleep that causes you to wake up as if you had been drugged. No, drugs are not the problem. It is the narcotic of loneliness. It is the inebriated feeling of raising your children alone. It has robbed the passion, and now it is after the respect. It is trying to destroy all of the various relationships involved. Too much weight for one to carry alone. They look in the eyes of the one who said, "I do" and say to themselves, "You didn't!"

I hope this book is provocative. I hope that it challenges you to become involved in the details. I hope it has challenged you to stop saying, "Go ask your father," or "Go ask your mother."

It is my prayer that the partnerships of marriage would again touch and agree and challenge the devils that are after our children. It is when we who are married gang up on the enemy that he has to flee. It is a tragedy for those who have a partner to be required to live as if they had none.

Can the effects of your presence be felt in your home? If something were to happen to you, write down what your children would miss from you. Look at the list. Is there anything there that extends beyond things? That is your net worth as a parent.

What is on that list? I cannot see it, but you can. Your children cannot see it, but they will feel the effects of it. It is an assessment of the total assets that you have invested in your children. If you are not proud of what you see, then stop it. Take off your white sheet and quit being a ghost in your own house. Children do not want you to haunt them; they want you to help them!

It's not just the children who need you. What can you do to revive the one who has been depleted trying to do it all? Maybe an apology would be a great place to start. Don't stop there; take over something that needs to be done with the children and do it! They are so thirsty for you. All they really need is you.

Many men and women have missed the one chance or opportunity to be a part of their children's lives. Later they ride in on white horses and try to play the role of a parent at a time that the child has outgrown the need. There are some things that cannot be recaptured. It is imperative that we alert one another and help keep each other on guard that parenting children is a temporary job with long-term benefits.

Those moments that have the unfortunate habit of coming right in the busiest part of your life are so precious that they will never be reduplicated. How can you maximize those moments? It is not easy. Time management helps. Terms that we hear all the time like "spending quality time" have almost become clichés. Yet they are still true. I think that times of open heart communication cling to the heart like honey sliding down the walls of a jar.

So I say to you, make it count. Whatever it takes, do it. It may require a day off every now and then. Maybe going to where the phone doesn't invade your privacy and spending a moment acting like a child with a child who is about to be an adult. They are transforming before your eyes. When life slows down and you are more available, they will not need the attention that you try to pay later. They need you now.

So my friend, whatever you do, do not be a stranger in your own house. Make sure that a hug doesn't seem strange. A good night hug or kiss seasoned with some wise counsel over a huge hot dog makes memories that last longer than we do.

A ghost is a fleeting shadow of a departed person whose only presence is a glimpse that passes so quickly that the beholder is not certain it was real. Slow down, friend. Let them know you are not a shadow; you are not a thump that passes in the night. You are not a ghost parent. Let them know. In spite of imperfections and flaws, you are real!

Get involved by increasing your presence gradually so that you do not send anyone into shock, yourself included. Sometimes when people have become accustomed to something being done one way, even if it is wrong, the change is difficult—partially because they are afraid to believe that it will last. So be gentle.

It will be a healing and a renewal for the over-stressed parent to be relieved. It may even strengthen your marriage for you to become more involved in your children's lives. Sometimes it is a matter of taking a greater interest. It really doesn't have to consume your time to be effective with the children.

There are few things more painful than the feeling of being alone. It is a feeling of alienation so intense that it is restrictive and emotionally crippling. There is no aloneness like the aloneness that exists when you are not really alone. The loneliness of not having anyone to discuss issues with regarding the children—I mean someone who isn't grunting discombobulated answers from behind a *Wall Street Journal*.

The feeling of aloneness is more palatable if it is accompanied by an empty room. It is disheartening to look around you and know that you are too married to be a single parent but too single to have a participating partner.

Have you ever just needed someone to be there, just to break the silence or relieve the tension? Sometimes it is as simple as taking the children out for yogurt or ice cream. It is providing a sabbath for someone who just needs a break for a moment. It doesn't have to destroy your goals or ambitions. It can be simply a pleasant distraction from the perils of day-to-day demands. If you have a tendency to be under-involved with your children, ask yourself some essential questions.

What good is it for us to achieve and acquire all these accomplishments and lose the family that we are trying to secure? Is it enough to provide things if we do not provide emotional and societal support? Have you realized what a premium is placed on the attention of the parent who evades the children? That parent's elusive attention epitomizes for many the true affirmation that causes the human soul to soar.

My prayer reaches out to both parents. You do not have to be a bad parent to be a distracted one. Many times it is a pattern that was started in your own childhood in which you defined parenting as a single parent activity. That idea can be based on your own childhood experiences. In fact, many good parents are oblivious to their own lack of participation in the lives of their children. They often replace affection and attention with provisions and protection. These are wonderful, but in the mind of a child, a smile is more nourishing than a half-eaten steak.

I pray for the dutiful, committed parents who find themselves torn between career demands and domestic responsibilities. I know how hard it is to be there for everyone and wonder, *When will I find time for myself?* My prayer is that you do not become increased with goods and become impoverished in the area of relationship. It is hard to balance, but perhaps I have helped to illuminate some areas of concern and thereby headed off possible snares of the enemy.

It is my prayer that you do not limit your role models to the ones in your own past, but broaden your borders to allow the Word of God and the people of God to assist you in acquiring options for involvement with your children. Mostly I pray that you will not be eaten up with guilt but instead motivated by love. All else will fail. Love alone will always prevail over inexperience, insensitivities and all other human frailties.

I also pray for the towers of strength who have held the domestic reins of the house singlehandedly. You are to be commended. You will probably remain unsung heroes—unsung by the children who tend to jockey for the attention of the elusive parent; unsung by society who assumes that you had more help than you did; and unsung by yourself, who lies down every night listing what needs to be done rather than appreciating how much has already been accomplished.

You are the champions who sit behind the scenes when touchdowns are made. You are the invisible fingers that stroke the pianos at recitals. Your tired legs are the ones that leap the hurdles at the track meet. For wherever your children go and whenever they succeed, you are there.

We salute you for countless hours of counseling, encouraging, praying and believing when all else failed. To circumvent all the negative statistics that permeate our society, God sent no angel. Neither did He send prophets. He sent none of His eloquent preachers. To change the children He sent the parents who care and share and give.

And every now and then they stand with their backs to the wind and their faces to the sun. They stand valiantly and grandly, and occasionally they stand alone. For all of this the world says, "Thank you!"

Discussion Questions

1. As evidenced by our Scripture portion for this chapter, God places great importance on children. As parents, our children must have top priority in our lives. On the lines below, list three ways you already plan your time to give priority attention to your children and their needs:

_____

_____

_____

2. Now think about conversations you have had with your children and hints that they may have given you to indicate areas where they would like you to give them more time or nurturing. Focus on one of these areas, and plan a way to meet this need. Outline your plan on the lines below.

_____

_____

_____

3. Jakes states that some parents "think their responsibility ends with the provision of money. Generally guilt drives them to spending an incredible amount of money as compensation for their absentee parenthood." Have you ever tried to compensate for the lack of time you spend with your children by buying them something instead? Describe what you did, and tell how it made both you and your child feel as a result.

_____

_____

_____

4. The author also says that it is difficult for those of us who had ghost parents not to become one. Describe some of the memorable, happy times you remember spending with your own parents.

_____

_____

_____

5. If you cannot recall happy times with your parents, tell how you have planned to include memory-making experiences in your relationship with your own children.

_____

_____

_____

6. During a family time together, ask each member of your family to propose one activity that everyone can do together. List these activities—and the times you will schedule them—on the lines below.

_____

_____

_____

7. The author says, "My prayer is that you do not become increased with goods and become impoverished in the area of relationships." On the lines below, give the name of each family member. Beside each name, describe the benefits that person has brought to your life as a family member.

_____

_____

_____

Shape Your Destiny Activity

A LETTER TO GOD

Materials: Stationery, envelopes, pencils.

Give each family member a piece of stationery paper. Explain that today each family member will write a letter to God, expressing three things that makes that person happy and three things that makes that person very sad.

Give each family member an envelope and ask them to fold their letter, place it in the envelope and seal it. Explain that you will hold the letters for three months. During that time each member should pray about the things they put in the letter. They should thank God for the things that they listed that made them happy, and ask God to give them more opportunities to feel happy like that. They should each pray about the things that made them sad, and ask God to show them ways to change those sad moments into happier times.

At the end of the three months, gather the family together again, and ask each family member to read his or her letter aloud. Give each family member time to express the ways God answered their prayers regarding both the happy and sad times. If there are still unresolved sad issues facing a family member, discuss ways to help that person find happier ways to interact. Discuss how other family members can help each person find ways to interact in happier, more positive ways.

Prayer

*Father, I thank You for the life of each person in my
family. I pray that You will help me to remember that
my children's needs are more important than the
busyness of my life. Help me to find ways to meet each
need and to nurture each child to become the fully
functioning adult that You created that person to be.*

*Father, each of my children is a special blessing to
me. I thank You for each one, and for the unique quality each adds to my life and to our family's existence.*
[Now thank God for each person by name, listing the
unique qualities of each person and praying for each
person's specific needs.]

*Teach me, Father, to make each day with my family
count. Show me how to help each of my children
become everything that You designed that person to be.
Help me to nurture each in such a way that I enable
each child to reach his or her destiny in You. Be my
Source of strength, my Teacher, my Guide and my
Wisdom.*

*Help me to show my children "the praises of the
Lord, and his strength, and his wonderful works that
he hath done…that they might set their hope in God,
and not forget the works of God, but keep his commandments" (Ps. 78:4, 7, KJV). In Jesus' name, amen.*

CHAPTER 11

Never Alone

GOD HAS ANOINTED YOU TO RAISE YOUR CHILD. HE HAS EQUIPPED YOU FOR THE JOB. HE KNEW YOUR CIRCUMSTANCES WHEN HE ENTRUSTED YOU WITH A HUMAN LIFE, AND HE GIVES YOU THE GRACE TO PERFORM WHAT HE HAS CALLED YOU TO DO. THAT KNOWLEDGE GIVES CONFIDENCE TO THE FAINT OF HEART AND THE WEARY IN WELLDOING. IT IS NOT SO MUCH THAT WE HAVE CONFIDENCE IN OUR OWN HUMAN ABILITY, BUT THAT WE KNOW OUR GOD IS ABLE TO GIVE WISDOM WE NEED TO BE EFFECTIVE.

For this cause we also, since the day we heard it, do not cease to pray for you, and to desire that ye might be filled with the knowledge of his will in all wisdom and spiritual understanding; that ye might walk worthy of the Lord unto all pleasing, being fruitful in every good work, and increasing in the knowledge of God; strengthened with all might, according to his glorious power, unto all patience and longsuffering with joyfulness; giving thanks unto the Father, which hath made us meet to be partakers of the inheritance of the saints in light: who hath delivered us from the power of darkness, and hath translated us into the kingdom of his dear Son: in whom we have redemption through his blood, even the forgiveness of sins.

—COLOSSIANS 1:9–14, KJV

God is with you in the nightmares of your life.
He will rock you to sleep in the bosom of His love
and cradle you in the palm of His auspicious hand.

One of the greatest myths in our culture is centered around people. We have a tendency to believe that if we are surrounded by people, we are not alone. But the truth of the matter is that people can surround you, even engulf you with accolades and entourage, and you can still feel alone.

It is not the reality of aloneness that is so painful—it is the *feeling* of being alone. That feeling can overwhelm you when people who once received you have now ceased to affirm you for one reason or another. Perhaps you failed to live up to their expectations, and now they are ignoring the person that they used to affirm.

I know you may not believe it, but people do change. Often it's without warning, and you may suddenly find yourself alone. It may not be a physical desertion, rather it may be an emotional or attitudinal change. But it still creates an aura of alienation. Many people spend their lives relentlessly trying to be accepted so that they may feel a part of someone else. It seldom works.

Neither the wealthy nor the poor are exempt from feeling alone. Both the attractive and the homely have been affected by loneliness. Many times it results from being around people whose motives are questionable. Any time another person's soul does not rest at peace in our relationship, that relationship ceases to minister to my needs. Whether guilty or imagined, the lack of trust leaves a wariness that sends a warning to my spirit that I am alone.

Many times depression comes from the feeling of being "in this thing" alone. No matter whether the aloneness is a test, a trial, a dilemma or a condition, if I feel that I have been forsaken, it brings on depression.

The prophet Elijah, a powerful man of God, hid under a tree in a state of depression over what he had lost. Later he ended up in a cave wishing he were dead simply because he thought he was going through a crisis alone. Have you ever found yourself under a tree or in a cave despairing of life itself?

> But he himself went a day's journey into the wilderness, and came and sat down under a juniper tree; and he requested for himself that he might die, and said, "It is enough; now, O LORD, take my life, for I am not better than my fathers."
>
> —1 KINGS 19:4, NAS

This is a word you must receive. He who could have been mightily used of God almost forfeited his destiny by allowing himself to succumb to a false sense of alienation. Elijah failed to look outside of his sphere and realize that God never leaves anyone alone. The help you receive may not be the help you expected to get. It may not come from the source you wanted to get it from, but trust me, you are not alone.

Look at Elijah's plea to God: "O Lord, take my life!"

Now there is euthanasia for you—he doesn't want to take his life; he wants God to do it for him. He wants assisted suicide from God. God is not in the business of helping men escape their destinies. He is in the business of helping men fulfill them.

Elijah was functioning under the misguided myth that he was left alone.

> Then he came there to a cave, and lodged there; and behold, the word of the LORD came to him, and He said to him, "What are you doing here, Elijah?" And he said, "I have been very zealous for the LORD, the God of hosts; for the sons of Israel have forsaken Thy covenant, torn down Thine altars and killed Thy prophets with the sword. And I alone am left; and they seek my life, to take it away."
>
> —1 KINGS 19:9–10, NAS

If Elijah were a singer, he would have sung, "Nobody knows the trouble I've seen." He believed he was completely and totally alone. Maybe you have felt alone like Elijah—alone as you raise your children; alone in the night. Have you ever felt hot, stinging, bitter tears cascading down your face because you felt as if there were no one to whom you could turn? Tragically you don't have to be a single parent to feel that way. Any time you are overwhelmed, overworked and underappreciated, depression's elevator can ascend into your heart and bring you down.

It is no wonder the Bible says, "Where there is no vision, the people perish" (Prov. 29:18, KJV). For anytime you fail to see available help you become discouraged. But you must understand that God has help available for you, and it is all around you. It may not be the traditional help of a spouse, but there are surrogate fathers and mothers whose wisdom and love can mend the breach of an empty void with your children. Many times if it doesn't come from the source we expect, we give up as if God were limited to one channel of expression. God is more diverse than that. He has many ways to get help to you.

He provides people in your life that He uses to strengthen and bless you. Never allow pride to blind you from seeing an opportunity that God created to bless you. Needless bitterness and loneliness can be eradicated if you will open your heart to the plans of the Lord. He has so many ways to meet your needs.

One of my prayers is, "God, give me creative thought." The world was created by the declaration of creative thought. People who have creative thought are always successful because they do not allow a vacuum to exist in their minds. You are only as limited as you believe yourself to be. I dare you to see every test as an opportunity to exercise creativity. In short, find a way!

When Ruth the Moabitess was gleaning in the fields, Boaz saw her and spoke to the reapers.

> When she rose to glean, Boaz commanded his servants, saying, "Let her glean even among the sheaves, and do not insult her. And also you shall purposely pull out for her some grain from the bundles and leave it that she may glean, and do not rebuke her." So she gleaned in the field until evening. Then she beat out what she had gleaned, and it was about a ephah of barley.
>
> —RUTH 2:15–17, NAS

Boaz knew that Ruth was a single woman with many needs. In essence he said to the reapers, "Ruth the Moabitess is behind you catching the wheat you leave behind. Since we know she is in need and too proud to ask, leave a handful on purpose." He intentionally arranged for her to receive blessings, thus providing for her needs. The reapers left her a blessing where she could receive it.

In the same way God provides for His own. He uses people, making them available to you so that you will not suffer loss. Always realize that the blessings come from God. Had Boaz not spoken to the reapers they would never have blessed Ruth on their own. So we thank the people whom God uses, but we praise the Lord.

He will cause people to want to bless you. He will cause them to take notice of you. He will bring you into a blessing you had no right to receive. I like to say, "He did me a favor." Has God ever done a favor for you? He has done it for me, and if you trust Him, He will do it for you. I challenge you to allow God to stir you into believing He will bless you. He will fulfill your needs and minister to your lack.

He will provide someone who doesn't mind helping you through a tough time. It may be someone who baby-sits for your children occasionally. Or He may send someone your way with a material blessing such as groceries or money. But thank God, He has people He will use to bless you so that you will be able to survive the challenges you face.

There is another truth so simple and yet so true that it has kept my heart from fainting in the day of my adversity. I can remember that when I was a small child I had occasional nightmares. Once or twice they were so severe that I climbed in bed with my parents so that I could sleep. It wasn't that I thought my parents could destroy the monster I had conjured up in my mind. I just didn't want to face the monster alone. I wanted my parents to be there in case I drifted into sleep only to discover the monster was still waiting for me. Just my parents' presence made me more comfortable.

Might I take this moment to remind you that you are not in this storm by yourself. God is with you in the nightmares of your life. He will rock you to sleep in the bosom of His love and cradle you in the palm of His auspicious hand. Even if the trouble is your own fault and all others have forsaken you, God has promised, "I will never leave you nor forsake you." What a promise and a privilege to know that you are not alone.

God has anointed you to raise your child. He has equipped you for the job. He knew your circumstances when He entrusted you with a human life, and He gives you the grace to perform what He has called you to do. That knowledge gives confidence to the faint of heart and the weary in welldoing. It is not so much that we have confidence in our own human ability, but that we know our God is able to give wisdom we need to be effective.

I have always asked God for help. I ask Him to give me the word of wisdom for my parenting.

Each of my children is different from the others. While one child may require firm discipline, another just needs tenderness and affirmation. Only God's wisdom will be able to tell a parent when to administer discipline and when to administer tenderness. You may be able to reason with one child, but another you must command with great authority. The anointed word of wisdom is the word that is effective. God's Word will not fail. It will get great results. Ask Him for wisdom. He will give it to you in great abundance.

> If any of you lack wisdom, let him ask of God, that giveth to all men liberally, and upbraideth not; and it shall be given him.
>
> —JAMES 1:5, KJV

Asking God to help you will remind you that you have a heavenly parent to whom you are submitted. You honor Him by not trying to resolve your problems on your own. You are acknowledging Him as the final authority when you ask Him for wisdom. Listen intently for His voice. He speaks subtly but powerfully. I must warn you that a stress-filled mind deafens the ears from hearing the voice of God. So calm down and wait. When the time is right, He will give you clear guidance and direction.

Knowledge gives you information, but wisdom gives you application. Many people have great knowledge. Some have received it from textbooks and some from observation. Knowledge is important, but wisdom is essential. It tells you how to apply what you know. Knowledge without wisdom is incomplete. Ask God for wisdom for the situations you are dealing with now. One word from Him will heal it all.

Ask Him for prophetic insight so you can help prepare your children with a vision of their future. I do not mean manipulation. Many parents want to control their children's outcome. That is not right. You are to guide them into what God reveals to be their destiny. If you see something they do not see, allow the Holy Spirit to reveal it to them. You cannot make your child a doctor just because you want him to be one. If God reveals to you that your child will be a doctor or a preacher, just provide that child with the tools and the opportunity necessary. Allow God to do the convincing. Your child will not resent God—but he could resent you. Sometimes it is not the motives that cause conflict, rather it is the methods. Be careful; you are dealing with the destiny of one of God's chosen. This is a matter of great delicacy.

The task would be too great for any of us, single or

married, if it were not for the presence of God. He is there to assist you in the challenges of life. He is your assistance when you feel overwhelmed. Allow Him to assist you by seeking His counsel, by speaking His Word into your children's lives and by holding onto godly values in this contemporary age.

I know there are days all of us feel as though we are in over our heads. But when those days arise and courage seems to wilt, remember that God's grace is upon you for these moments. He will strengthen you against all odds. Some of you have always had someone else to rely on. But now you are facing the challenge of raising your children alone. Are you alone? Not really. You never were. God has been there all the while. And the same God who brought you through all of your earlier challenges is waiting for you to acknowledge Him in your present situation!

Many of the blessings that are upon you will pass to your children. It is a blessing to have wise parents. Wise parents pass their reasoning and mentality on to their offspring. It creates a generational blessing. We have heard much about generational curses, but we need to understand generational blessings. If a drug-filled mother produces a drug-addicted child, then why can't a spiritually regenerated mother produce a child that has been spiritually impacted from birth? That might sound preposterous, but it is not at all.

> For he shall be great in the sight of the Lord, and shall drink neither wine nor strong drink; and he shall be filled with the Holy Ghost, even from his mother's womb. And many of the children of Israel shall he turn to the Lord their God.
> —LUKE 1:15–16, KJV

The angel spoke a word of prophecy to Zacharias

regarding the birth of his son to Zacharias' aged and barren wife. Zacharias was left mute after this word, and he didn't speak until the birth of the child. He was smitten with silence because he would not believe what the angel said. Elizabeth, an excited, pregnant, senior citizen, had no one with whom to share her joy. She was with child—and yet alone.

When her cousin, Mary, who was carrying our Lord, came to the door, Elizabeth was so excited by Mary's greeting that her baby leaped in the womb and was filled with the Spirit even as the angel had said. In spite of the fact that Elizabeth's husband did not believe and perhaps did not support her in this pregnancy, God blessed her on the basis of her faith.

A blessed parent can produce a blessed child. The Bible says that there were none greater than John the Baptist. Christ eulogized him at his funeral and applauded his character. When Christ says you are a great man, I believe you are a great man.

> But what went ye out for to see? A prophet? Yea, I say unto you, and more than a prophet. For this is he, of whom it is written, Behold, I send my messenger before thy face, which shall prepare thy way before thee. Verily I say unto you, Among them that are born of women there hath not risen a greater than John the Baptist: notwithstanding he that is least in the kingdom of heaven is greater than he.
> —MATTHEW 11:9–11, KJV

The favor of God is with you as a parent. His hand is there to bless you if you will but trust Him. If John, who was birthed in a chaotic environment, was blessed by God to yet rise to heights unheralded in his generation, what can God do for you and yours? It is

God's design to bring strength out of weakness and power out of pain. I challenge you now to allow Christ to equip you with the tools you need to become what God would have you to be as a single parent. I am persuaded that God's blessings are about to break out in your life as never before.

> Let not mercy and truth forsake thee: bind them about thy neck; write them upon the table of thine heart: So shalt thou find favour and good understanding in the sight of God and man. Trust in the LORD with all thine heart; and lean not unto thine own understanding. In all thy ways acknowledge him, and he shall direct thy paths. Be not wise in thine own eyes: fear the LORD, and depart from evil. It shall be health to thy navel, and marrow to thy bones.
>
> —PROVERBS 3:3–8, KJV

Do not lean to your own understanding. He will give you His wisdom as you travel onward in faith. Faith is a walk in the dark with a firm hand planted in the hands of a God you cannot see. It is asking Him to do what you cannot articulate, and being able to smile in the wind because you know in your heart that He is going to do it.

Faith is having the grace to accept the challenges and the struggles of your course, but doggedly and tenaciously searching for the victory within the victimized. You are the vessel God has chosen to labor with Him in forming the character of the next generation. You may not live long enough to see all of your fruit, but your teachings will reach the third and fourth generation. It will be your standards that shape your family for years after you are gone. Do it with dignity and character. It is your contribution to the next age.

It is reported that every revolutionary group from the Ku Klux Klan to the Nazi regime impacts constituents by indoctrinating them at early ages. It has been said that the hand that rocks the cradle rules the world. I am praying for your hands. For through your hands there may be a child that will discover the cure for AIDS. Through your hands may come a president or world leader that will bring harmony in place of bigotry and righteousness to our government. You do not know whom you are raising. All you know is that a thousand diseases could have destroyed the child before birth. But God blessed you with the life of that child. There is a purpose for that child being in your life and being raised under your hands. Cultivate that which is good, and shun that which is evil.

No wonder the enemy wants to overwhelm and discourage you. When he gets you, he gets two for the price of one. He affects you and the child in one blow. Tell the devil no! He will not get a two-for-one sale here. You will guard with all diligence what God has entrusted in your hands. Charge your children with faith and power. They are the future. We are already the past. We can live forever through their beating hearts. Our eyes can see the future through their faces. We can taste the exotic foods of foreign countries through their lips. Wherever they go, we go also. They are our children, our seed and our destiny.

> As arrows are in the hand of a mighty man; so are children of the youth. Happy is the man that hath his quiver full of them: they shall not be ashamed, but they shall speak with the enemies in the gate.
> —PSALM 127:4–5, KJV

If my children are my arrows, they are my defense. They are my defense against emptiness. They are my defense against building a house that no one will inherit. They are my defense against having no hand to hold when death comes to carry me home. They are my defense against anonymity in the next generation. My quiver is full. I have five children. Five is the number of grace. What a grace to have children for tomorrow.

So as a father I raise my bow. I have five arrows. I will sharpen them all that I can. I will point them toward the heavens and hope that they land amongst the stars. I will raise my bow. Even if I am shot, I will raise my bow. I will lift it above my past, my pain and my fears. These arrows—my children—are my defense. In them my pain has purpose; it becomes the catalyst that makes me pull my bow back the hardest. I will raise my bow. I will not trust my children's teachers to raise it. I will not trust my church to raise it. I will raise my bow. They are my arrows. I will aim high, pull hard, focus my vision and let them go sailing—sailing in the wind.

If they fall to the ground and plummet to earth having never touched what I aimed for or expected them to touch, never let it be said that they failed because I didn't raise my bow. So I say to you as you face the uncertainty of the future and move gallantly past the pain of yesterday, never for one minute think that you are alone. Stand up straight, square your shoulders, and raise your bow. Who knows? You might be the one that hits the stars with your arrows.

You may never be famous, but your children might be. Few would recognize Martin Luther King's mother. Few would recognize the names of Jacqueline Kennedy Onassis' parents. Even fewer would know Colin Powell's parents. But somewhere behind the curtains, in the shadows of the stage, there is a face, a hand, an apron, a father or a mother who said, "I will raise my bow."

I leave you single parents with the words of an old, favorite hymn. It is for you and all parents who ever felt they were all alone. It is a word of comfort from the Father sent to the parents of children who need to be reminded that in the nightmares of your life you may climb into your Father's ample arms and find peace.

> I've seen the lightning flashing,
> And heard the thunder roll;
> I've felt sin's breakers dashing,
> Trying to conquer my soul;
> I've heard the voice of my Saviour,
> Telling me still to fight on;
> He promised never to leave me,
> Never to leave me alone.
>
> The world's fierce winds are blowing
> Temptations sharp and keen;
> I feel a peace in knowing,
> My Savior stands between;
> He stands to shield me from danger,
> When earthly friends are gone;
> He promised never to leave me,
> Never to leave me alone.
>
> No, never alone! No, never alone!
> He promised never to leave me
> Never to leave me alone.

As I come to the close of this ministry to you, I do it with mixed emotions. I am glad that you allowed me to share my heart with you. I am sad that it is time to close. Yet I know that I must release you from the sanctity of ministry to fulfill your destiny in Christ. Stand tall and look up—the Lord is with you. I cannot say what you will face, no more than I can declare my own adventures. But I can remind you as days pass and life moves on, you are not alone.

Just when you are feeling low, God will send someone to cheer you. Look for them; they are the reapers who have been instructed to leave a "handful on purpose" for you. They are sent by God to bless you. Some will be on the bus you ride. Some will meet you at the water cooler at work. Others are sitting in the barber shop or beauty shop, waiting for you. Expect them to come just when you thought you could take no more.

I cannot tell you where God left them, but I certainly can declare that He did leave them. In fact, look back over your life. He has been leaving you little signs and blessings all the time. He has not run out of blessings. He is the same God. He brought you through before—He can bring you through this.

So keep your eyes open and your heart strong. Raise your bow and shoot your arrows. Prepare your children as though they were king's kids. Because they are—they are the King's kids!

I will close with the words that were given to Moses' mother as she received her son who had been resurrected from the chilly waters of a river that could have consumed him. The daughter of Pharaoh said it so well.

> And Pharaoh's daughter said unto her, Take this child away, and nurse it for me, and I will give thee thy wages. And the woman took the child, and nursed it.
>
> —EXODUS 2:9, KJV

I can say it no better. It is simply saying what God has said to you. "Take this child, nurse it, raise it, nurture it! Whatever it takes to strengthen this child, I will supply. I will give you thy wages." What does that mean? It means that God will bless you as you serve Him by caring for what He has created and entrusted to you.

He is speaking through this passage to those who feel as though life has not been fair: "Go ahead, take this child. Raise it. I will pay thee thy wages." Get ready. Get ready. Get ready! The wages are coming your way!

Discussion Questions

1. The author says, "It is not the reality of aloneness that is so painful—it is the *feeling* of being alone." Describe some of the feelings of being alone that you have experienced.

   _____

   _____

   _____

2. Feeling alone can cause depression, just as it did in the life of Elijah. From this chapter we learned that Elijah failed to look outside of his sphere and to realize that God never leaves anyone alone. Sometimes our help comes from the most unexpected sources. Think about the times you have felt alone. Who came along to help you in those times, and what did they do to help?

   _____

   _____

   _____

3. This chapter tells how God provided for the needs of Ruth by providing "handsful on purpose." He led Boaz to tell his reapers to drop some grain intentionally, providing her with food for herself and for Naomi. How has God dropped "handsful of blessing on purpose" to meet a need you may have had?

   _____

   _____

   _____

4. Our chapter quote tells you that you are the special person God chose and anointed to raise your children. That means you are the perfect person for the job! Take the time to think about the positive contributions you can make to the life of each

of your children that no one else could make. On the lines below, list the name of each child. Beside each name, describe a special characteristic you possess that is of specific help to that child.

_____

_____

5. Jakes says, "Knowledge give you information, but wisdom gives you application." Much of the wisdom contained in the Book of Proverbs is of great help to a parent. Find three verses in Proverbs that give you wisdom you can use in the nurturing and discipline of your children.

_____

_____

6. The author tells us that God will give us prophetic insight to help prepare our children with a vision of their future. What specific giftings and abilities have you been able to observe in your children that you believe are prophetic "glimpses" into the futures God has for them? (Example: A child who shows deep compassion for the needs of other children may be gifted for a helping career such as medicine, teaching, etc.)

_____

_____

7. Wise parents pass generational blessings on to their children. On the lines below, list the blessings you would like to pass along to your children. Be specific by listing specific blessings for each child if you can.

_____

_____

_____

Shape Your Destiny Activity

Producing a "This Is Our Family" Puppet Show

Materials: Hand puppets.

During this activity, your family will write a puppet show describing your family in each of the three following scenes:

1. Your family one year before today

2. Your family as it is today

3. Your family one year from today in the future

Let family members write the story any way they choose, concentrating on showing the personality and emotions of each family member. Be sure it is a collaborative effort and not directed by one family member only.

Provide a hand puppet for each family member. Decide together whether each member will portray himself or herself or assign another family member to portray each person.

Practice your puppet play, and then share it with friends, neighbors or extended family members. Gather as a group after the play has been shown to discuss various parts. Discuss how it accurately depicted your family, and how you can make any changes that may have been brought to light as needing to be changed as a result of the play.

Prayer

Father, thank You for the awesome privilege—and the awesome responsibility—of raising the children that You have given to me. Thank You that You have taken the shattered dreams of our lives and have given us a second chance, a new beginning. Teach my family and me to use our past to fertilize the future. Help us to use the pain we have experienced as the fuel that strengthens our prayers, our hopes and our dreams of a better day.

Help me to lift myself from my problems so that I am able to lift up my child with positive reinforcement and personal contact. Teach us to be overcomers—not just survivors or victims of our circumstances. Let the scars of my past failures become the stars of great victories that are birthed out of the challenges in our lives. Help each of my children to be a modern-day Jephthah—an overcomer who knows he is the child of the King.

Help me to teach my children a healthy self-image that is not built on the opinions of others. Let me model the truth that Your presence can fill every empty place in our hearts, bringing "joy in the morning" (Ps. 30:5). May I follow Your leading so closely that my children will rise up to honor me as they grow. Help me to structure their lives with discipline and order, and to structure my own with Your comfort and rest.

Prayer

If You bring a mate into my life, may it be someone who will "marry" my children as well as me. Close my eyes to anyone who could not be the parent my children would need, the helpmate and support You planned for me. Prevent me from becoming a "ghost parent" by becoming so distracted by career and other things that I neglect the care and nurturing of the little ones You have given to me.

Above all else, remind me continually that You have promised, "I will never leave you nor forsake you." Fill my life with Your wisdom. Help me to hear Your promise that says, "Take this child, nurse it, raise it, nurture it! Whatever it takes to strengthen this child, I will supply. I will give you your wages." In Your name, amen.

OTHER BOOKS BY T. D. JAKES

Daddy Loves His Girls

Woman, Thou Art Loosed!

Can You Stand to Be Blessed?

Water in the Wilderness

Why?

Naked and Not Ashamed

Loose That Man and Let Him Go!

VIDEO PACKAGES BY T. D. JAKES

MANPOWER I

Healing the Wounded Man Within

MANPOWER II

Marriage: Bonding or Binding

Forgiveness: Final Frontier

Make This House a Home

For more information on tapes, books and other products, please write or call:

T. D. JAKES MINISTRIES

Potter's House
6777 West Kiest Blvd.
Dallas, TX 75236
1-800-BISHOP-2

DADDY LOVES HIS GIRLS

BY T. D. JAKES

Daddy Loves His Girls is the next step beyond T. D. Jakes' *Woman, Thou Art Loosed!* It explores the fatherly love God has for His daughters. It offers hope for women with painful pasts, and it gives men the courage to love their daughters. Every mother should see it. Every daughter should hear it. Every father should say it . . . Daddy loves His girls.

Available at your local Christian bookstore or from:

Charisma House
600 Rinehart Road
Lake Mary, FL 32746
1-800-599-5750
Fax: 407-333-7100
www.charismahouse.com

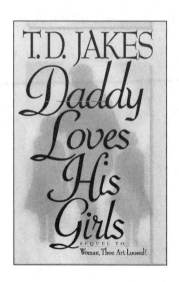